THE BUSBY BABES

Max Arthur is a lifetime supporter of Manchester United. He is this country's leading oral historian and the author of the classic work, *Forgotten Voices of the Great War*. His most recent work *Last Post – The Final Words from our First World War Soldiers* was the biggest selling history book of 2006.

THE BUSBY BABES

MEN OF MAGIC

MAX ARTHUR

MAINSTREAM
PUBLISHING

EDINBURGH AND LONDON

First published in Great Britain in 1998 by
MAINSTREAM PUBLISHING COMPANY
(EDINBURGH) LTD
7 Albany Street
Edinburgh EH1 3UG

An edition of this book was published in 1983 under the title
The Manchester United Aircrash

ISBN 9781845963415

A catalogue record for this book is
available from the British Library

Typset in Galliard and Helvetica

Printed and bound in Great Britain by
William Clowes Ltd, Beccles, Suffolk

CONTENTS

Acknowledgements   7

Foreword by Sir Alex Ferguson   9

Foreword by Matt Busby   11

Preface   13

Introduction   15

Peter Howard: The First Report   31

Harry Gregg   37

Bill Foulkes   53

Dennis Viollet   63

Johnny Berry   81

Albert Scanlon   87

Ray Wood   97

Jackie Blanchflower   105

Kenny Morgans   111

Bobby Charlton   115

Jimmy Murphy   123

Roger Byrne   133
Geoff Bent   139
Tommy Taylor   141
Liam (Billy) Whelan   147
Eddie Colman   151
David Pegg   157
Mark Jones   161
Duncan Edwards   167
Omo and Daz   171
Bobby Robson   175
Nat Lofthouse   179
Norman Williams   183
The New Dawn   189

ACKNOWLEDGEMENTS

I would like to thank all those at Manchester United who helped with the preparation of the first edition of this book, for without their kindness and co-operation it would not have happened.

In this revised edition, I am again grateful to Cliff Butler, for his assistance with the players' statistics, and Mike Maxfield, the manager of the United Museum, for additional details on several of the players.

I want to thank all those at News Team International in Manchester, who scoured their photographic archives time and time again, and Lisa Bell at Express Newspapers Syndication. Both did an outstanding job and I am most grateful to them. I am also grateful to Colorsport, who supplied additional photographs.

I must again record my appreciation to all who gave me personal accounts of their experiences. All have enriched this book.

FOREWORD

It seems like only yesterday when what I believe to be the greatest season in Manchester United history culminated on the pitch at the magnificent Nou Camp stadium. On 26 May 1999, the most dramatic European Cup final of all time created the most memorable two minutes in our club's history, with an equaliser by Teddy Sheringham and then the winner seconds later by Ole Solskjær to seal an unbelievable victory over Bayern Munich, clinching for us the Treble in the process. The fact that the UEFA president missed both goals, as did a crestfallen George Best, speaks volumes as to how the fortunes of United changed in the blink of an eye.

Unbelievable scenes followed. A vivid memory for me is of Peter Schmeichel, in his final game of an illustrious United career, doing cartwheels in celebration. The players that night elevated themselves to the status of legends with their never-say-die attitude and hunger to overcome the odds.

That night will be added to the long list of great European matches Manchester United have been involved in, not least the triumph of Sir Matt Busby's team in the 1968 final, led by the legendary Sir Bobby Charlton. The 1999 game had added poignancy for me in that it was played on what would have been Sir Matt Busby's 90th birthday, and it was against a team from Munich, a place that will forever be associated with Manchester United and the 'Busby Babes'.

Almost 50 years ago, as I write, Manchester United suffered the worst tragedy in its history when the aeroplane carrying the great young team built by Sir Matt Busby crashed on their third attempt at take-off at a snow-covered runway in Munich. Much has been written over the years about the huge loss of life and the enormous gulf this left in a team that had promised so much for the future. The average age of the side which won the championship in 1955–56 was just 22, and, led by Sir Matt Busby and Jimmy Murphy, they should have gone on to achieve greatness, both at home and abroad. It speaks volumes for their talent that it would take a revitalised Busby a decade to attain the level of European dominance his Babes could have achieved, with victory over Benfica in the final in 1968.

I have now been at the helm of Manchester United for over 20 years, and still this period of our history resonates throughout the club – from the tea ladies in the boardroom down to the ground staff. Every player who has come through the system here in my time, no matter if he is a high-profile signing like Wayne Rooney or a promising 15 year old at our academy, knows the history of Munich and what a loss to the club it was.

However, we do not just mourn their loss, we celebrate them as the players they were then and speak in pride of what they had achieved already. I can think of no better way to pay them tribute than with the fine collection of interviews Max Arthur has woven together in this book, which tell the story of this set of iconic players from the point of view of those who knew and played with them and who cherish their memory still.

SIR ALEX FERGUSON

FOREWORD

From the 1983 edition,
The Manchester United Aircrash

Twenty-five years ago Manchester United suffered a great tragedy when the Elizabethan airliner on which we were returning from a match against Red Star Belgrade crashed on take-off from Munich, where the plane had stopped to refuel. Aboard were 17 of the finest players the club has ever known. Eight of them died in the crash and two others, though surviving, were never to play football again. The crash also took from Manchester United three of its most loyal servants, Walter Crickmer, Bert Whalley and Tom Curry.

Max Arthur has spoken at length to the survivors and to the friends and relatives of those who died, and from these interviews, sometimes serious, sometimes humorous, he has created a portrait of each player. Their character and their skills are recalled by those who played with and against them. The survivors tell their own story.

Much has already been written about my own part in the formation of the Busby Babes. I am therefore delighted that this book also records the magnificent work done by the largely unsung backroom boys and in particular Jimmy Murphy.

This is a unique and fitting tribute to an unforgettable team. Those who never saw them play will, I hope, be made richer by this book. Those of us who remember them so well will not be saddened by it, but will be reminded that they were men of magic.

MATT BUSBY, 1983

PREFACE

On a quiet, sunlit, mid-November morning I sat up on the terraces of Old Trafford. There were no crowds, no one training and the only sounds came from a motorised mower. It was hard to believe that this ground, which had seen such excellence and absorbed such tragedy, could be so still. Yet even in its stillness it maintained its unique aura, for there is no other ground like it. Old Trafford has seen and survived it all. Its very soul is indestructible.

Old Trafford pulsates with life and vitality at every home game. The supporters of United are passionate and committed and have an intense loyalty to a club they love. For them there is no other club. There is only United.

United has a history steeped in excellence. Since the war, few clubs can boast names like those that have graced Old Trafford: Carey, Delaney, Pearson, Rowley, Byrne, Colman, Edwards, Taylor, Charlton, Law, Best, Giggs, Cantona, Rooney and Ronaldo span four generations of football greatness. The greatest of them all, however, was the 21-year-old prince, Duncan Edwards. I believe that he played for potentially the greatest side this country has ever known. This book is about that team. Their story is told by the players who survived the Munich disaster, and the stories of those who did not return have been written from interviews with their relatives, friends and those who played with and against them.

Sir Matt Busby evolved the youth scheme that was to create the Busby Babes of the 1950s. I have not, however, written the story of Sir Matt; this has been done so well before. The tribute to him is that his influence is felt in every page of this book.

I have written a short history of the years immediately preceding the Munich crash and also a brief account of the accident. The major part of the book, however, is about the 17 players who were the Busby Babes. Although the book was written 25 years ago and now revised, our affection for the Busby Babes remains as high as ever. Now there is a new generation to learn of their magic, for their legend will never fade. In the intervening years Sir Matt, Jimmy Murphy, Johnny Berry, Peter Howard, Jackie Blanchflower, Dennis Viollet and Ray Wood have all passed away, but their spirit remains.

MAX ARTHUR, 2008

INTRODUCTION

Unless there were beauty and grace
in them, they would be powerless
to win our hearts.

ST AUGUSTINE

The 1957–58 season started well for the Busby Babes. Although it was obvious to a wise onlooker that the United team was not fully mature and therefore had much potential to look forward to, they were undoubtedly ready and confident to take on anyone. With 27 league games completed, United were lying in fourth place and felt assured that the six-point difference between them and Wolves could be eroded. They had already scored 68 goals that season by the time they came to Highbury on 1 February 1958. No one could know that for many of the players it would be their last game before a British crowd. The side that played Arsenal that day was the same as that to play the following Wednesday at Red Star Belgrade: Gregg; Foulkes, Byrne; Colman, Jones, Edwards; Morgans, Charlton, Taylor, Viollet and Scanlon.

After ten minutes a well-placed pass from Viollet gave Duncan one of his typical goals. Running in from outside the penalty area, he picked up the ball and slammed it into the net with such power that Jack Kelsey was left dumbstruck. Shortly afterwards Albert Scanlon made one of his tantalising runs covering half the pitch. He spotted Charlton and centred to him, Bobby driving the ball home without hesitation. Just before half-time, a superb cross-over move by Albert Scanlon and Kenny Morgans, typical of United's highly creative style, produced a pass from Morgans which was slotted in by Tommy Taylor to make the score 3–0.

By the second half it looked as if United could take an early train home, and so it was to seem until half an hour before the final whistle. Suddenly the game ceased to be predictable and took on a bizarre dimension. It was almost as though Arsenal knew that they had to extend the Babes to produce a magical exhibition of football one last time, for within three minutes Arsenal had levelled the score. Herd scored first and Groves a minute later. Then, before the excitement had died, Bloomfield, dashing in like a man late for the bank, glanced the ball off his forehead past a bewildered Harry Gregg.

United reeled momentarily, then, in their own in-domitable fashion, recovered their composure and began to reassert themselves. A superb run by Bobby Charlton, combining with Albert Scanlon, led to a cross that was headed home by Dennis Viollet to make the score 4–3. The hysterically excited crowd felt that this surely must be the end, before some astute play between Eddie Colman and Kenny Morgans gave Tommy Taylor his second goal of the afternoon to make it 5–3. Unbelievably Arsenal kept coming and an inspired run by Tapscott produced a fourth goal for them. The final few moments saw both teams hammering away, but then the final whistle sounded. All effort was spent. The crowd rose as one to salute two wonderful teams who, exhausted, left the field arm in arm. Manchester United and Arsenal created a game that day which will always live in the memory of the thousands of people who saw it. It was what football should always be: passionate, unpredictable, exciting and exhausting – but, above all, magical.

The following foggy Monday morning United had an uneventful flight to Belgrade, stopping at Munich to refuel. Although they had an important match ahead of them against Red Star, they knew that in order to reach the European Cup semi-final they merely had to draw. United had beaten Red Star 2–1 at Manchester. After Saturday's amazing game, United were quietly confident. It was the confidence of young boys who had grown to men and who now had the world before them.

They had a wealth of history behind them too, for since the war United had gone through an evolution. They had evolved from a top-class side of the late '40s to this remarkable side. Their coming together was the result of a decision taken by United, for shortly after the end of the Second World War the ex-Liverpool, Manchester City and Scottish international Matt Busby was asked to take over as manager. He was to take over a near-bankrupt club at the bombed-out Old Trafford ground and create from the ashes some of the greatest players and three of the greatest teams that British football has ever seen. There is no doubt that where football and footballers are concerned, Matt Busby was a genius.

Once he had re-established the pre-war players and added a few signings of his own from other clubs, he was able to see his first great team emerging: Crompton; Carey, Aston; Anderson, Chilton, Cockburn; Delaney, Morris, Rowley, Pearson and Mitton. This powerful and mature side beat Blackpool in the 1948 Cup Final which is believed by many, even today, to have been the greatest final of all time. By the end of the following season, United's finances were looking a little healthier, for they had made just over £50,000. The ground, too, was beginning to look less like a bomb site.

Looking forward to the following decade, Matt realised that however good the side he had was, there was nothing in reserve. Many of his players were approaching the end of their careers. There was very little money to spend in the transfer market, and the only option left open to him was to create a youth policy. He gave the task of initiating this new way of life in British football to his assistant manager, Jimmy Murphy, a former Welsh international. Jimmy and his assistant Bert Whalley, the coach, and Tom Curry, the trainer, travelled the length and breadth of the British Isles searching for and signing on the most promising 15- and 16-year-old schoolboys. Despite this nationwide search, many were found on United's own doorstep and needed little persuasion to play for such a club.

Matt created a family atmosphere for these boys in which they could grow both as footballers and as individuals. He also handpicked the landladies who would look after the boys, some of whom had never left home before. The club was then still small enough to be looked on as a family. Matt had on his staff men who had seen much of life and who would understand the needs of young footballers. Apart from Jimmy Murphy, Bert Whalley and Tom Curry, the secretary of the club was the diminutive and gentle Walter Crickmer, with his young assistant Les Olive. Bill Inglis was assistant trainer and Arthur Powell was the colts' trainer. Ted

Dalton was the physiotherapist and Joe Armstrong was the chief scout. In the office Alma George ruled supreme and the staff was completed by two ladies in the laundry who affectionately became known as Omo and Daz. This was the small but intensely loyal firm under whose guidance Matt's Babes were to mature to such greatness. So successful was Matt's policy that between 1951 and the Munich air crash, United bought only three players: Johnny Berry for £25,000, Tommy Taylor for £29,999 and Harry Gregg for £23,500. Just as in the case of the youngsters taken straight from school, all three signings were handpicked by members of the United 'family'.

Slowly and patiently the youngsters were coached through the youth side in which they matured gently until they were ready for promotion to the Central League side, where they would learn something of the rigours of professional football. After a spell with this side, most were ready to take a place in United's first team. After graduating from the Matt Busby 'Academy', very few failed to succeed in the first team.

Matt was well aware that with so many good players coming on there would be many clamouring for a place in the senior team. This was very much part of his scheme, for he knew that constant competition would keep all his players fighting for a place. He had obviously remembered Napoleon's adage: 'The strength of an army lies in its reserves.' Here were 22 young boys, full of competitive family spirit, all eager to eat round a table that had only 11 places. Apart from Tommy Taylor, who could usually command the centre-forward position, the rest of the forwards would have to fight for their places. Each one of them would have been able to find a place in any other club and not have to put up with such competition, but they chose to stay with United.

A look at the forward line that was available to Matt for selection would make any league manager undeniably envious: Berry, Morgans, Whelan, Charlton, Viollet, Scanlon and Pegg. The half-back line of Colman, Jones and Edwards could also include the remarkable Jackie Blanchflower, who was quite capable of playing in any of those positions. At left back Roger Byrne had always kept out Geoff Bent, who was one of the most outstanding backs in the game. Matt Busby had created a highly adaptable and multi-talented side. The skills and talents of each member of this team are shown in their individual stories which follow.

This constantly maturing combination of players won the 1955–56 league championship with 60 points (this was in the days when only two points were allotted for a win). Their closest rivals in the league table, Wolves and Blackpool, were both 11 points behind them. What United needed was a fresh challenge and more excitement, for they wanted to be tested. There was only one place – Europe. The talents of the Babes were now to be pitted against opposition of immense skill and experience.

In United's first year in Europe they were to play some of their greatest ever games, on one occasion destroying Anderlecht by an incredible ten goals to nil, Dennis Viollet knocking in four of them. It was an exhibition of magical football. The two games against the experienced Athletic Bilbao produced football of a quality seldom equalled in United's history. Certainly Whelan's goal in Bilbao which cut the opposition's lead to only two goals must rate among the greatest of all time, and the final goal by Johnny Berry at Manchester, following a magical run by Tommy Taylor, produced one of the greatest ovations seen for a United goal. That night Manchester went wild. In the European Cup semi-final United's feet were placed firmly back on the ground by Real Madrid with such masters as di Stefano and Gento. Though disappointed at losing, United were always ready to learn a lesson and start again.

For the second year running they had won the league championship, this time with 64 points, and they had reached the FA Cup Final against Aston Villa. Unfortunately, an injury to Ray Wood during the match left United, in those pre-substitute days, with only ten men. Jackie Blanchflower took over in goal and Duncan Edwards did the job of two men for the rest of the match, but it was not quite enough and Aston Villa won 2–1. Matt said after the match, 'Don't worry, boys, we will be back.'

The game against Red Star was tough and erratic. In the first half United played much as they had in the first half against Arsenal, with plenty of fast, creative and flowing football. In under two minutes the centre half, Spajic, failed to clear properly and the ball hit Tommy Taylor, rebounding to Dennis Viollet's feet. Dennis was never a man to miss such a golden opportunity. Shortly afterwards Charlton had a goal disallowed, but then, almost out of revenge, he turned on the power and pace that was his hallmark. In the 28th minute he thundered home a left-foot drive and, as an encore, three minutes later hit a right-foot shot past the goalkeeper, Beara. At half-time United were 5–1 ahead on aggregate.

In the second half Red Star were determined not to lose face and fought like tigers, willed on by a vast and partisan crowd which intimidated the referee, Karl Kainer. Two minutes into the half Kustic scored from 20 yards. Three minutes later, Foulkes was pulled down by a falling Red Star player but Herr Kainer decided that Foulkes was the one who had committed the foul and so awarded a penalty against United. Tasic scored from the spot. In a rare moment of anger over a decision against Colman, Duncan Edwards had his name taken. This gives some indication of the state of feeling among the players, for Edwards seldom remonstrated with a referee. The players now suffered the consequences of some fierce tackling by Red Star and Duncan hurt his ankle. Harry Gregg was also hurt and Kenny Morgans was kicked on the thigh.

Red Star threw everything they had at United in the dying minutes of the game, and moments before the final whistle a shot from Kostic hit the head of Viollet, who had dropped back to help the besieged defence, and spun into the net. Red Star needed one more goal for a replay – but somehow United kept them out.

In their last two games United had put on a tremendous exhibition of creative football, scoring eight goals and conceding seven. In both cases, although cut, bruised and exhausted, they had come through victorious. Henry Rose, one of the journalists to die in the crash, wrote of the club he loved: 'HEROES ALL. None greater than Bill Foulkes. None greater than Bobby Charlton, who has scored 12 goals in the 11 games he has played since he came into the side at inside right on 21 December. But all 11 played a noble part in this memorable battle.' A banquet followed the match and Matt allowed the lads an extra couple of hours afterwards to relax and have a drink. The next morning, still tired, the team took off for

Manchester via Munich. They were due in Manchester early that evening. The chartered Elizabethan aircraft was carrying 38 passengers and a crew consisting of Captains Thain and Rayment, Radio Officer Rodgers and a cabin staff of William Cable, Margaret Bellis and Rosemary Cheverton. As Thain brought the aircraft to Munich he descended through dense cloud which obscured the runway almost until the last minute. As the plane came down it sent a great wave of spray high above the cabin windows. At 13.11 Thain switched off the engines. All the players and press men ran to the airport buildings for a quick cup of tea, and as they ran some of the lads snowballed the refuelling crew – who could not reply as they were on top of the wings with their fuel pipes, and there was insufficient snow where they stood. Captain Thain later checked the wings for snow and was satisfied that they did not need cleaning.

At 14.19, just over an hour after landing, Captain Rayment requested permission to taxi to the runway. Eleven minutes later, having given clearance, the airport control tower heard from Rodgers that 609 Zulu Uniform was 'rolling'. Forty seconds later, when the aircraft was on 'Full Power', both pilots detected an uneven engine note. In a flash, Captain Rayment whipped the throttles back and called 'abandon take-off'. Permission was granted for them to taxi back for a second attempt, and both pilots agreed that on this attempt they would open the throttles more slowly. At 14.34 the plane once more came to a halt half-way down the runway. Opening the throttles more slowly had not worked. This time Captain Rayment spoke over the intercom to reassure the passengers that it was only 'a technical fault'. By 14.39 the plane had taxied back to the airport buildings. There seemed little likelihood of United reaching Manchester that evening. The match against Wolves, who were top of the table, was very much on their minds, and, what they all needed most was a good day's rest on Friday. There was much talk and nervous laughter among the team and press men while they grabbed something to drink. Frank Swift, the gentle giant who had kept goal for England and Manchester City and was now a journalist, was the ideal person in moments of stress. He took his overcoat from his massive frame and draped it round the diminutive Eric Thompson of the *Daily Mail*. This caused a laugh and a lifting of the spirits, which was the effect Frank had wanted to achieve.

Everyone was expecting to have to wait at least a couple of hours, yet within minutes – and certainly before some people had ordered their drink – a call came for everyone to return to the aircraft. This created a sense of unease among the passengers.

Prior to the call to return, the B.E.A. station engineer, William Black, had spoken with both pilots and listened to their explanation about 'boost surging'. Black explained that this was not an uncommon feature at airports such as Munich which were at sea level. They agreed that the throttles should be opened even more slowly than before. Neither pilot considered that the wings needed sweeping. Thain also dismissed the idea of an engine retune.

As the passengers climbed aboard, Peter Howard (whose story follows) took a photograph of the team, the last ever to be taken. The doors were closed, only to be reopened to let in Alf Clarke, who had been to phone his newspaper about the possibility of staying in Munich overnight.

Captain Rayment sought permission from the control tower to taxi. This was given. Shortly afterwards the control tower called back: '609 Zulu Uniform – München Tower – wind two nine zero – eight knots – cleared for take-off. Cleared to runway two five – QNH one zero zero four – over.' A request for clearance to line up was made by Rayment two minutes later, and clearance was given. Forty seconds after 1500 hours the control tower heard from Rayment: '609 Zulu Uniform is ready for take-off.'

At 15.03 Rodgers informed the tower that they were 'rolling', and less than one minute later the final message came from the doomed Elizabethan: 'Munich – from 609 Zulu Uniform'. What followed was an indistinguishable 'howling, whistling noise', with a low background noise. The final few seconds are related by Captain Thain.

'The needle of the air speed indicator was flickering, and when it indicated 117 knots, I called "V1" and waited for a positive indication of more speed. Captain Rayment was adjusting the trim of the aircraft. Up to this point, although I had not looked out of the cockpit, I had not experienced any feeling that the acceleration had been other than normal under the circumstances. The needle wavered at 117 knots and then dropped by four or five knots. I was conscious of the lack of acceleration. The needle dropped further to 105 knots and wavered around this speed. Suddenly Captain Rayment called out, "Christ, we won't make it."

'All this time my left hand had been behind the throttle levers. I raised it and banged the throttles, but they were fully forward. I believe Captain Rayment was pulling the control column back. He hurriedly called, "Undercarriage up." I selected the up position, gripped the ledge in front with both hands and looked forwards. The aircraft's passage was smooth, as if we had become airborne, and it looked as though we were slowly turning to starboard. I remember thinking that we couldn't get between the oncoming house and the tree. I lowered my head and the aircraft crashed.'

Thain was right. The plane did not get between the house and the tree. After leaving the runway and crashing through the perimeter fence, it went across a minor road and struck the house. The tail and one of the wings were torn off, and the house caught fire. The rest of the aircraft, spinning and sliding out of control, careered on. The port side of the flight deck was crushed against a tree. One hundred yards past the house, the starboard side of the fuselage struck a wooden shed which housed a petrol lorry, which immediately exploded, bursting into flames that rose to a great height. Still, part of the wrecked plane careered on until it came to a halt 70 yards from the petrol tank.

Captain Thain, severely shaken but unhurt, gave the order to abandon the aircraft and then began to fight the fires with a small extinguisher. He did his utmost to free Captain Rayment, who was trapped in the cockpit, but his efforts were in vain. Rayment eventually had to be cut free. He was the first injured person Thain was to see, but there were to be others – many fatally so.

From the moment Manchester heard the news of the crash a dark mantle of gloom hung over the city. Men wept openly in the streets – people could not believe it had happened. At first, there was no news concerning who had perished or who had survived, but as the evening wore on and things became clearer, the list of casualties filtered through to the waiting crowds. This is the final list of those who died in the crash or later in hospital:

Players

Geoff Bent – Reserve Left Back
Roger Byrne – Captain and Left Back
Eddie Colman – Right Half
Duncan Edwards – Left Half
Mark Jones – Centre Half
David Pegg – Outside Left
Tommy Taylor – Centre Forward
Billy Whelan – Inside Right

Manchester United Officials

Walter Crickmer – Secretary
Tom Curry – Trainer
Bert Whalley – Team Coach

Journalists

Alf Clarke – *Manchester Evening Chronicle*
Don Davies – *Manchester Guardian*
George Follows – *Daily Herald*
Tom Jackson – *Manchester Evening News*
Archie Ledbrooke – *Daily Mirror*
Henry Rose – *Daily Express*
Frank Swift – *News of the World*
Eric Thompson – *Daily Mail*

Crew of the Aircraft

Captain K.G. Rayment – Co-Pilot
W.T. Cable – Steward

Other Passengers

B.P. Miklos – Yugoslav Travel Agent
Willie Satinoff – United Supporter

The following survived:

The Club

Matt Busby – Manager
Johnny Berry
Jackie Blanchflower
Bobby Charlton
Billy Foulkes
Harry Gregg
Kenny Morgans
Albert Scanlon
Dennis Viollet
Ray Wood

Journalists

Ted Ellyard – *Daily Mail*
Peter Howard – *Daily Mail*
Frank Taylor – *News Chronicle*

Passengers

Mrs Vera Lukic and child
Mrs B.P. Miklos
Mrs N. Tomasavic

Crew

Captain J. Thain
Mr W. Rodgers – Wireless Operator
Margaret Bellis – Stewardess
Rosemary Cheverton – Stewardess

'We got it through word of mouth. Only two things ever interrupted school: the crash and the Cuba crisis. You see, Eddie only lived 300 yards away; he was our local star. I used to go to his grave every week.'

MIKE SWEENEY, PICCADILLY RADIO DISC JOCKEY,
WHO WAS 12 AT THE TIME

'I remember the coffins coming back – the roads were black with people, and everywhere there were white handkerchiefs. It was the grimmest day Manchester ever had.'

UNITED SUPPORTER

'At Old Trafford, dozens of people on the car park, just waiting; and among them many young faces begging to be told it was not true. Inside, Les Olive, a still, pale mask beneath his reddish hair, standing beside a mound of telegrams, coping manfully, because all the men had gone.'

TONY STRATTON SMITH, AT THAT TIME
A YOUNG JOURNALIST WITH THE *DAILY SKETCH*

'The next day everyone seemed to be wearing a red and white scarf. I wore mine to school where they were fussy over uniform, and made it clear that young ladies did not go to football, let alone advertise the fact, but for once no one said anything. This was my way of expressing what it all meant to me. No one in the bus spoke, though some people said they were sorry just because I wore a scarf. We went to the ground – I don't know to this day why we went. The plane carrying the coffins was late and it was due at eight o'clock. The police had to come and tell us that the coffins would not arrive until 11.30 and that they had to reroute them. But we waited; we owed it to them.'

ANNE SMITH,
UNITED SUPPORTER

PETER HOWARD

The First Report

'The pilot tried a third take-off. It was like going down a cobbled road.'

JACKIE BLANCHFLOWER

After the crash Peter Howard, the *Daily Mail* photographer, crawled out of the aircraft on his hands and knees, pulling Ted Ellyard with him. Ellyard told Howard that he could not see. As soon as they were outside, Howard pulled and ran with Ellyard until they were 30 yards clear of the plane as he was worried in case it exploded. Ellyard was still complaining that he could not see, but when Howard examined his eyes, he found they were caked in mud! He heard Harry Gregg shouting at anyone he could find to help the injured. He saw Gregg bring out Mrs Lukic and then come out with her baby. Howard considered Harry Gregg to be the hero of the hour.

Howard and Ellyard went back into the aircraft a number of times to assist in the rescue and to reassure the injured. They helped lever the wheel from Kenny Morgans and to prop Ray Wood against the bags containing United's strip. Howard then helped recover Frank Taylor, whom he considered beyond help. He clearly remembers seeing the wireless operator, Rodgers, running around, still trying to extinguish the flames. Howard then went with Captain Thain to prepare a list of those injured and killed.

Less than one hour after the crash, and still in a state of shock, Peter Howard had the presence of mind to phone the news desk of the *Daily Mail* to pass the following report. This is his full report.

> I am phoning the terrible news. Manchester United's plane has crashed at Munich. We were just taking off. We had only just got off the ground. Can you hear me? I'm all right. I feel a bit wobbly. Tell my wife I'm okay. Please let her know. It's all a bit mixed-up at present, but Bobby Charlton, Albert Scanlon and Ray Wood are injured and have gone to hospital. Most of the crew are safe. Harry Gregg, the United goalkeeper, looked to be okay when I saw him just after the crash, but I haven't seen him since. We had a pleasant trip from Belgrade. Everyone was happy and laughing and joking because we were coming home and United were in the semi-final.
>
> It was snowing when we landed at Munich. We went off for refreshments and then we went back to the aircraft to continue the flight. I was sitting in the second row of seats on the starboard side of the aircraft with Ted Ellyard, who wired my pictures of the game from

Belgrade. When the pilot tried to take off, there seemed to be some kind of slight fault with the engines. He stopped. Then he tried a second take-off. That didn't seem satisfactory, so he taxied back to the apron to get things checked up. It was on the third take-off that we crashed. I think we were about the end of the runway, only a bit above the ground.

The plane suddenly appeared to be breaking up. Seats started to crumble up. Everything seemed to be falling to pieces. There was a rolling-over sensation and all sorts of stuff started coming down on top of us.

There wasn't time to think. Everybody seemed to be struck dumb. No one cried out. No one spoke. Just a deadly silence for what could only have been seconds. But it seemed a long time. I can't remember whether there was a bang or not. Everything stopped all at once. I was so dazed that I just scrambled out. Then I found Ted Ellyard and I were still together. We found a hole in the wreckage. We crawled out on our hands and knees.

As soon as I got clear, my first instinct, quite frankly, was to run away. I was terrified. But I managed somehow to stay put. I turned round and there was big Harry Gregg, who had also managed to get out. He seemed unhurt too. Anyway, his voice was in working order for he was shouting, 'Come on lads, let's get stuck in.' That got us going. Gregg, Ellyard, two stewardesses, the radio operator and myself went back into the wreckage. It was a terrible mess. It made me want to shut my eyes. I was conscious of the same deadly silence that was there just before the crash. We turned to and did what we could.

I saw Captain Thain, one of the crew, get hold of a hand fire extinguisher; he started putting out small fires. It looked as if all those who had been sitting in the forward part of the plane were the lucky ones who got out. The luckiest of all were in the backward-facing seats, sitting with their backs to the crew's cabin. I looked round to see if there was anyone I knew. I saw Captain Rayment, a member of the crew, trapped in the cockpit, but later he was released.

A Yugoslav woman passenger and her small baby were pulled clear by Harry Gregg and the radio operator, Rodgers. I couldn't see anything of my friend Eric Thompson, the *Daily Mail* sports writer and I'm just realising what an awful thing it is. Everybody had done all they could just before I left the wreckage. It suddenly came to me that I had taken some pictures before take-off. I looked for my camera but I couldn't find it. There was wreckage all over the place. It covered an area of more than 150 square yards. Part of the airliner's engines had gone forward some distance and hit a small house, which burst into flames, but the fuselage did not catch fire – that was the fuselage part that I was in – apart from the small fires which Thain put out.

I wish I could say what had happened to the rest of the party. I didn't see Matt Busby after the crash. Now I am thinking about my wife,

Pam. She is bound to be worried. Please tell her I am safe. I can't tell you what my phone number is here. They're refusing to accept calls. I think I am perfectly all right but they are insisting I go into hospital. I'll have to go now but the sooner I can get back to Manchester the better. My mind seems stunned. I wish I could tell you it was not so bad. I'm afraid some have gone for good, but it was all over quickly. There was no panic. It makes me feel proud of United. These lads were my friends. I have been everywhere with them. I shall never forget this. I shall have to pack up now, they want to drag me off to hospital. See you soon.

Even though Peter Howard was stunned by this catastrophe, he remained remarkably calm and lucid. At no point in his report does he exaggerate or give any misleading information about the casualties. He reported only what he saw and believed to be true.

Peter Howard died on 12 February 1996.

HARRY GREGG

*'When you have a guy like that who climbed
back into a burning plane to help his
friends, you've said it all.'*

NAT LOFTHOUSE

After the Red Star match we played cards until the early
morning, when we set off for the airport. Digger Berry
somehow lost his passport and immigration would not let
him through until eventually it was found on the aircraft.
When we boarded the plane the lads carried on the card
game we had begun the previous evening. I'd won quite
a bit of money and they were ribbing me for not wanting
to play. There was a poker school and a rummy school
going on in different parts of the plane. I told them I'd
play after we'd taken off from Munich.

   When we came into Munich to refuel we did not see
the ground until we were about to touch down because
of the very low cloud. As refuelling took a little while, we
were able to get off the aircraft and have coffee and buy
some odds and ends at the terminal.

After we had all reboarded we started to take off. I was looking out of the window and saw the wheels locking, slewing the plane round. Captain Thain said that there was a technical fault and apologised for the delay, saying he would try another take-off immediately. This did not work either, and the pilot braked and took the plane back to the terminal. We all got off the plane again and went back into the terminal buildings, where we all sat around waiting for the plane to be got ready again. I remember buying some Players cigarettes and discussing with the others how we would get back by boat via the Hook of Holland. Nobody took this suggestion seriously and we all had a good laugh, despite the fact that there was a certain amount of tension amongst us. The first two attempts to take off had been quite unnerving and for me possibly more frightening than the third time, as I had been watching the wheels sticking in the slush.

When we got back into the plane some of us were quite nervy. I saw the steward actually strapped into his seat when we got on, which was not very reassuring! Alf Clarke was late getting back to the plane and we had to wait for him. I was quite worried by this time. I sat very low in my seat, opened my trousers and my collar and sank down into the seat with my legs up. I tried to crack a few jokes but Johnny Berry, who was sitting near me, was too anxious to be amused by them and said he thought we would all be killed. Billy Whelan, who was sitting next to him, said, 'Well, if that's going to happen I'm ready for it.'

We set off once again. I remember looking out of the window and seeing a tree and a house passing by and suddenly we were passing places we had not done before. Everything went black all of a sudden and sparks began to fly. I was hit hard on the back of the head and

I thought the top of my skull had been cut off. The plane seemed to turn on its side, sort of upside down. There was no crying. There was just silence and blackness and then for a second there was daylight again. I thought I was dead, so I sat there quietly and a strange idea passed through my mind. I remember thinking I had had a great life and a wonderful family and I couldn't speak German!

There was a great hissing noise all around me and I realised that I was still alive and lying on my side in my seat. I unfastened my seatbelt and began to climb out. There was still no sound apart from this tremendous hissing. Captain Thain suddenly appeared holding a small fire extinguisher and told me to run for it. I was about to take his advice when I heard a child crying, so I crawled back into the wreckage. People outside were shouting, 'Get out, get out, run for it!' I shouted to them to come back as there were people alive inside. I found the baby and started to carry it out. The radio operator took the child from me and I went back into the debris and found the mother, but she was in a bad condition. I found Albert Scanlon, who was badly hurt, and I tried to get him out too, but he was trapped by his feet and I couldn't move him. Peter Howard, the *Daily Mail* photographer, was with Albert, keeping him company.

I ran round to the back of the plane and found Bobby Charlton and Dennis Viollet lying in a pool of water. I thought they were dead and dragged their bodies, like rag dolls, into the seats which had been thrown about 20 yards from the plane. I started calling for Jackie. As I searched for him I saw the tail end of the plane ablaze with flames. I found Matt Busby, who was conscious but holding his chest in pain. He was propped up on his elbow and did not look too badly hurt although his foot was broken. I left him and found Blanchie, who was sitting up to his waist in water. Roger was close by him. Jackie's arm was bleeding badly, so I tied a tourniquet on it with my tie. I pulled so hard that I snapped my tie in half but managed to tie his arm with the bit that was left.

Suddenly a man in a long overcoat arrived carrying a syringe. I shouted to him to go and help the injured in the aircraft, but suddenly there were some explosions from the burning half of the plane and the force of them threw this doctor off his feet. He was a strange sight, falling on his backside in the snow, with his legs in the air, still holding that syringe in his hand.

I turned round and got the shock of my life, for there were Dennis and Bobby standing, just watching the fire. I was so relieved, as I had been sure that they were dead. Shortly after this, when it looked as though the rescuers had everything under control, I sank to my knees and wept, thanking God that some of us had been saved. I had never seen death before and never wanted to see it again.

Things began to happen fairly rapidly and Dennis, Bobby and I were put into a Volkswagen van. I sat in the front with Bill Foulkes, who appeared to have come through unscathed. Johnny Berry and Jackie were lying in the back with Matt; all were badly injured. As we set off, the driver was obviously in a great hurry and driving so rapidly that Billy felt something dreadful was going to happen. I remember him getting up and belting the driver, who appeared to take no notice; but he got us to the hospital.

In the hospital they gathered all the survivors together

and those of us who could walk were asked to identify the others. We were given some soup to warm us up but I remember that even that had a disinfected hospital smell. I remember hearing over the intercom in the hospital that we had lost Frank Swift. The whole atmosphere was so unpleasant and there was nothing that Foulkesy and I could do, and we decided to get out, although I had a cut nose which I did not want treated. As a result my nostrils are now of different sizes.

We went to a hotel in Munich, where the manager gave us each a warm coat and some other clothes. Somebody also gave us some whisky. I remember looking out of the bedroom window and seeing the snow piled as high as the cars. I thought about what the snow was burying at the airport.

Later at the hotel, we had dinner with the B.E.A. crew and Captain Thain explained to us what he thought had happened.

The following morning when I got up I was terribly stiff and so was taken back to the hospital, where they gave me an injection in my back. When this had been done I left the ward and went round to see all the lads. The following day Jimmy Murphy arrived and took Bill and me back to the hospital to visit the injured. Many of them were in a bad way and the hospital told us that 'Digger' Berry had only a 25 per cent chance of recovering. I remember Duncan, who was fairly ill, asking what time the kick-off was on Saturday. Foulkesy and I stayed together and followed each other all over the place.

There was one amazing angel who arrived at the hospital, and that was Jean Busby. She was magnificent, comforting and caring for everyone despite her obvious worries for her husband, who was lying upstairs gravely injured.

Jimmy decided that we should get back to Manchester as soon as possible, and since nobody seemed terribly keen on the idea of flying back we went back by train and boat, via the Hook of Holland. I remember on the ship having a terrible nightmare in which Mark and Duncan were driving an army wagon backwards towards me. They kept coming backwards, and even though I was screaming at them they ran over me. On the train from Harwich to London I was in a very nervous state and jumped every time the brakes were applied. Hubert Gregg, the actor, came to our compartment with his very attractive wife. He said he was a great follower of United and was very sorry to hear of the tragedy. To this day I regret that I was somewhat abrupt with him.

A few days after I got home I noticed that people were hiding the newspapers from me – they were trying to protect me from the news of Duncan's death. That brave boy who I had been speaking to only a few days before was now dead, and I couldn't accept it. I was so angry. For me that was the beginning and the end of Munich. After that I threw myself totally into my football. I could get out there and fight and shout and get rid of the pent-up emotions that boiled within me. It was the only thing that kept me on the rails.

The rest of that season was an anti-climax. The team, if one could call it that, was patched up by members of our Central League side so I was kept fairly busy, which was all right with me. Before the match against West Bromwich Albion, Vic Buckingham, their manager, had said, 'United are a wonderful side but we can have no sympathy – we'll beat them 6–0.' That spurred us on and it is a great compliment to our lads that we drew the match 2–2.

The Cup Final, which we lost, was something of an anti-climax, though I remember one amusing incident. We had been told not to chew gum at the pre-match presentation. I had forgotten about this and was chewing away as the Duke of Edinburgh came forward. I popped the gum into my hand, and then found myself shaking hands with the Duke with that same hand!

But I will always remember standing on that snow-swept airfield feeling helpless and alone. I will always feel a part of something great; the greatest club in the world. Maybe not always the best team, maybe they never were – but they were the most loved. They carried the passions of the people; they carried every schoolboy's dream of belonging to them. When I think of all the trauma throughout the years at Old Trafford and still I see the legions follow them, I realise that it did not all end on that airfield all those years ago. Those emotions are still there. What a tribute that is to United.

I came to United from Doncaster two months before the crash. I have many memories of those early days, but what immediately hit me when I arrived was the warm family atmosphere that emanated from the Boss downwards. The two trainers, Tom Curry and his assistant Bill Inglis, were a real double act. Bill with his big 'Schnozzle Durrante' nose was always smoking; he kept his cigarette concealed in the centre of his hand so that over the years his palm had become dark brown. Tom was a quietly humorous pipe-smoker. These two made a great combination and were a credit to Matt's ability in selecting his lieutenants. He knew how to use their own particular talents.

The boys loved Tom and occasionally used to steal his tobacco pouch and fill it up with cut-up condoms. On another occasion they blew up a dozen of them like balloons and tied them to Tom's hotel bed and round the lampshades. These were wonderfully childish tricks and only done because we loved him so much. For some unknown reason Tom and Bill always wore ice-cream coats. I suppose it was part of the set-up. Tom would always get us to train hard, but it could also be fun. I remember one day we lined up across the field, linked our arms and did the can-can. Down the tunnel and through the fog came Tom's pipe. He saw the performance and the joke. There was no screaming, no shouting; he just shook his head and, feigning disgust, turned on his heel and went back in. Such was our respect for him we just got on with the hard graft as soon as he had disappeared. I don't think we trained very hard in those days because we were playing two to three games a week. We didn't need to train. Some of those lads, especially the internationals, were playing 65 to 70 games a season. They never got stale. They were playing for different reasons in those days.

We felt it was a privilege to be playing for United, although they did work us very hard. We used to be sent 'up the back', which was a stretch of concrete around the pylons. If you could play football on that, you could play anywhere. Kenny Morgans always excelled on this surface. I think this was Matt's way of keeping us at a basic level so that we never forgot what type of team we were meant to be. We were never spoilt; our training equipment and match gear were never flashy.

Matt and Jimmy were hard taskmasters but fair. Matt was the great diplomat, keeping any trouble within the club and allowing only good news to filter through to the outside. No one ever crossed Matt. You adhered strictly to the rules so that everyone knew exactly where they were. You certainly never swore in front of the Boss. Later, when I was a manager, I used many of his techniques. As he always said, 'If they act like men, I treat them like men. If they act like boys, I treat them like boys.'

Adjusting to a new team is never easy, especially for a goalkeeper. United were very used to Ray Wood, who was a marvellous line goalkeeper with tremendous reactions, but I wanted to control the whole penalty area. I reckon that if I stayed on my line when the play was on the half-way line, if the ball was lobbed over our defence I would have handicapped myself by 18 yards. I worked out that the further I went forward the closer I was to the action. I have always felt that if you don't put the piano stool close to the piano, you can't play!

In my first game for United, against Leicester City, Matt had dropped five international players in order to try his new boys. Early in the game I came out for a high ball and knocked Duncan over. There was no criticism – it was just a case of the defence adapting themselves to a new keeper. The lads quickly realised that I was not going to stay on my line. We all adapted accordingly. As Roger Byrne said, 'Keep coming, big man.'

I remember vividly my first local derby against City when we drew 2–2. I was very pleased with my performance that day and at Piccadilly Station on the way home I bought 'The Pink 'Un'. In the paper was a cartoon depicting me tied to a totem pole with the lads whooping and dancing around me with tomahawks. The caption read: 'Have United bought a goalkeeper or an attacking centre half?' Matt thought this might upset me and assured me that I had been bought for my style of play. He could see the basis of a player's anxiety and relieve it with just a few laconic words. Players were selected at Old Trafford for what they had to offer, not to suit any fancy formation, not because you were a right back or left half or centre forward – Matt picked a team of 11 footballers.

Jimmy Murphy was also an astute psychologist. I remember once when I was not playing too well I went back to the club to train on my own in the afternoon. Jimmy saw me and told me in no uncertain terms to go home. 'I'm paid to do the worrying, you're paid to play,' he said.

Matt and Jimmy understood the players very well but their approaches were very different. At the team talk Matt would tap the table with two fingers, reinforcing his comments. He would point out the characteristics of the opposition which he knew in great detail. He would tell us to watch a certain player who came inside the back or one who was slightly suspect down his left side. He would never say a player was either good or bad but merely gave you a clear picture of him before you went out on to the field. He always said that if we were not capable of beating the team we were up against, we would not have come through those big gates to join United in the first place. We used to smile at this because there had never been big gates in our time! Finally, he would tell us to go out and enjoy ourselves and just play football, because that way the results would come. This was always done in a quiet tone.

Jimmy's approach could not have been more different. His talks were full of passion backed up by a repertoire of colourful language and unrepeatable expletives. I am sure that half our success in our early days in Europe could be attributed to Jimmy's approach to us prior to a game. He was obviously calling on his war-time memories when we played against Continental sides. I remember once in Europe, where Jimmy had been during the war, when he said to us, 'I've seen this bunch of ***** in action, I've seen what they did to your fathers – get out there and destroy them.' Then he said to us, almost under his breath, 'God bless.'

Some people regarded Matt and Jimmy as gods, but they were basically wonderful, warm people, full of an emotion which they cloaked – and we respected that.

It is not difficult to recall the lads because each one had such a strong personality. There was the reserve left back Geoff Bent, who was a charming, quiet fellow and a good player. He was a real footballer, and that is a compliment. He was a footballing defender. He could play left or right back – the potential was there to carry it. He was hard and cool. I remember he used to give driving lessons and did this once even with his foot in plaster.

Billy Whelan: don't be deceived by pictures of that slight-framed lad. He was a quiet charmer but as a player he was gold-plated. He could get past people but it wasn't speed that did it. I'm not sure that it was even skill. I don't know what it was but he just seemed to glide by them, and when they were beaten they stayed that way. He was gold and silk rolled into one. He was a genius.

Tommy Taylor – what a great handsome man he was. Full of life, full of running, always available, loved training, loved playing. In the air he was probably one of the best I've ever seen. I should know. I played against him.

Young David Pegg: here was a young boy who was England's winger and justifiably full of himself. He was floating on air when I met him. He was a nice fellow. He played with strength and pace. You could play a ball into any space and he would pick it up. He could go past defenders with the ball and cross it brilliantly.

Bill Foulkes: he was big, strong and brave. Anybody who picked a battle with Bill lost it.

As a player Roger Byrne had a great gift and was a great skipper. He was the personification of the team we played for. No one got out of line with Roger. He led through his intelligence and kept order well, but he was very much one of the lads. When I played against him for Ireland he appeared to me to be aloof, but I can assure you he was far from that. He had a mind of his own. I had the pleasure of staying at his home when I first went to United. I learnt then that, even more important than being a good player, he was a good man.

What a lovable man was Mark Jones – a really handsome man. Big broad shoulders, big wide forehead, blond hair, a trilby and a pipe. Mark Jones was Yorkshire through and through. He loved his country, his shire, his wife, his family, his dog and his budgies! Mark was as warm as a man could be with his feet planted firmly in the earth. How he loved to sing 'On Ilkley Moor Baht 'At' – in fact he never seemed to stop. For me he was the best English centre half of the day.

Eddie Colman was the nearest thing to the essence of Salford. He depicted everything that *Coronation Street* used to stand for – flat cap, duffle coat and scarf. One would think that he was on his way to work in the dock, not to play for Manchester United. When I was playing in goal I used to move in time with his body every time he advanced – he was hypnotic.

They are all legends now, but Duncan Edwards is the greatest legend of all. For him every race had to be won, every five-a-side, every game. He was potentially one of the greatest all-round players in the world. He was the most shy and retiring of men. He was obsessed by football.

What a pity there had to be an 'if' about any of those lads.

Two of the survivors never played again. There was Jackie Blanchflower, whom I remember as a schoolboy. He could play in any position from goal outwards. He carried this great gift from school to league football and through to international level. His best friend was Tommy Taylor. I remember when he was playing for Ireland and had to mark Tommy. He read him so well that he played Tommy off the field.

Then, of course, the old man of the team was Digger Berry. He was an old-fashioned winger. He could take on and beat anybody. He would never let his bone go to the dog. He was very brave and would certainly have a place in any team of mine. But, as I say, they were all great players – gifted giants.

They were all great to play with. I can always say that I was part of that greatness; part of the Manchester United family and proud of it. There are not many who can say that.

HARRY GREGG

Born: Magherafelt, 27 October 1933
League Debut: (for United) v Leicester City
  (Old Trafford), 21 December 1957
Full International Debut: v Wales (Wrexham),
  31 March 1954

Playing record with Manchester United

Season	Football League		FA Cup		European Cup	
	Games	Goals	Games	Goals	Games	Goals
1957–58	19		8		4	
1958–59	41		1			
1959–60	33		3			
1960–61	27		1			
1961–62	13					
1962–63	24		4			
1963–64	25					
1964–65						
1965–66	26		7		5	
1966–67	2					
Total	210		24		9	

Playing record with Northern Ireland

1953–54 v Wales
1956–57 v England, Scotland, Portugal, Wales, Italy,
  Portugal
1957–58 v England, Italy, Wales, Czechoslovakia,
  Argentina, West Germany, France
1958–59 v England, Wales, Scotland
1959–60 v England, Wales
1960–61 v England, Scotland

1961–62 v Scotland, Greece
1963–64 v Scotland, England

Also played in the Football League for:

Doncaster Rovers, Stoke City

BILL FOULKES

*'When the chips were down and there was
a battle to be fought, Bill Foulkes
was always in the thick of it.'*

DENNIS VIOLLET

Looking back to my time at Manchester United, what dominates everything else was the crash at Munich. I had always enjoyed flying and was never worried by it; we could have flown upside down through a thunderstorm and it would not have bothered me at all. But I remember some of the boys did not like it. Mark Jones was always apprehensive and Duncan was always sick.

Even though I enjoyed flying, having already had two unsuccessful attempts to take off from Munich I was somewhat uneasy when we started the third time. Even before we began to taxi I had settled right down into my seat with my head well below the top of it. I was facing the tail of the plane and had fastened my seatbelt so tightly that it was almost cutting me in half. I kept thinking they should not be taking off. That they were wrong to take off. How could they take off in all this snow?

Just about the time I felt we would be leaving the ground I suddenly heard three terrific bangs, and felt them too. The first one I think was when we hit the fence at the end of the runway, the second must have been when the pilot retracted the wheels and the third, the loudest of all, must have been when the plane hit the house.

I don't remember very much of the next few moments because everything was very confused. When my mind cleared I was still strapped into my seat and could see that the plane had apparently been cut in half. There seemed to be a huge hole on either side of the fuselage. I undid my seatbelt and walked straight through the hole in the plane. This was typical of me, as I only walk in straight lines. Some of the lads say that I played football that way too!

I must have walked 30 or 40 yards from the plane before I began to realise something had happened. My feet were wet and it was very cold. I remember standing with a group of people, mainly women, watching the ensuing confusion. I don't think anybody there had realised that I was part of it all. I'm not sure that I did either for a few more moments, and then it all came to me. What sticks in my mind is seeing the tail of the aircraft sticking up in the air with that bloody Union Jack on it. That seemed to be the first thing I saw and I began to make my way towards it. It was then that I saw all the debris and the seats thrown about all over the place, many of them with people still in them.

As I approached I saw Harry Gregg coming out of the side of the aircraft, his face covered in blood, carrying a baby in his arms. Harry was shouting, 'Hey give us a lift here! Give us some help!' I could see on the other side of the aircraft some of the people who had been thrown out. Matt Busby was there and Bobby Charlton, Dennis Viollet, Johnny Berry and Roger Byrne were all in the snow, still in their seats. Johnny was in a bad way and I could see by the way he was sitting that Roger was beyond help, but the others seemed to be all right. So I thought there was only Roger dead and a few injured. Jackie Blanchflower had been badly hurt, and although he was conscious, he was bleeding badly from the arm. I can't get over Harry's presence of mind. He tied Jackie's arm really tightly in order to stop the bleeding and it is quite possible that this action saved Jackie's arm and maybe even his life.

Shortly after that someone drove up in a Volkswagen van and Dennis, Bobby and I got Matt, who was in a bad way, into the back of the van and we set off for the hospital. I remember getting very upset with the driver. He seemed to be going far too fast and we were skidding all over the place in the snow. I could not have been thinking very clearly for I remember getting up and hitting him, trying to get him to slow down, but he didn't take any notice. He just got on with his job and got us to the hospital.

We must have stopped briefly because I remember Mrs Miklos being put into the van with us. She seemed to be quite badly hurt. I don't remember much when we got to the hospital except that they were all very efficient, so calm and organised you wouldn't have thought that there had been an accident at all. I recall being shown into a room and there was Johnny Berry and Captain Rayment, the co-pilot, and Frank Taylor, the journalist, all of them fairly badly injured. I didn't know what to do. I was nearly in tears at the time. Frank said, 'Don't you speak to the poor, Foulksey?' I went straight over and sat next to him on his bed. There he was, so badly injured, and yet somehow, had managed to get hold of a bottle of beer. I remember he was the last one to be released from hospital. He was there for weeks and weeks.

Harry and I, since we were unhurt, did not have to stay in the hospital, and so we were taken back to Munich where we stayed at a hotel for two days, being looked after by B.E.A. staff. We came back to the hospital during those two days. I assumed the rest of the lads were in another hospital. So I asked where it was. It was then that they told us, very gently, that there was no other hospital and that all the others had not survived. I just wanted to get out, to get away. I couldn't believe it.

Later, Harry and I went back to the scene of the crash, for some reason, and I remember there were some photographs in the papers the following day of us standing among the debris. We found Eddie's scarf and his cap and a ring belonging to Mrs Miklos.

Jimmy Murphy arrived in Munich shortly afterwards and arranged for us to return to Manchester. We travelled back by train! Jimmy had got us thinking about the game we had to play the following week and was doing his best to cheer us up and take our minds off what had happened. In the train there was a Chinaman walking up and down one of the coaches and I remember Jimmy telling him that we might need him for the team next Wednesday! I didn't enjoy the train journey, as every time it braked, I felt as though I was living through the plane crash all over again. On the way back Jimmy Murphy told me that I would have to be captain for the next game. He didn't say we'll make you captain or do you want to be captain, he just said you'll have to be the captain. This really worried me because I had never captained before and I was anxious after all the problems we had just gone through in case we'd be thrashed. I worried so much over the following days that I lost over a stone in weight. You see, people kept coming up to talk to me and all I wanted was peace and rest. I really wanted to get away. Harry Gregg played brilliantly in that match against Sheffield, but he must have been worried as well because he had lost a lot of weight too. When we got on to the pitch, he and I were like a couple of skeletons. Ernie Taylor was great; he worked like hell in that game – but then so did everyone else.

It is strange that up to the moment of the game I had been thinking so much about the boys and missing them, but when the game started all I could think about was that we simply had to win. There was no way that we could lose that match. There were thousands and thousands of people there, all willing us to win, and after a few moments I realised they were going to be right. I think the effect of this was felt by Sheffield Wednesday. I am sure most of them felt that there was no way they were going to win that game; they just went through the motions of playing and we won that match 3–0.

Although I was completely exhausted, I could not sleep for days afterwards, nor could I eat. I knew I was not well; it was as though I had flu. I was drained. I know Jimmy felt I should not continue playing and I was certainly playing very badly, but he had the sense to leave the decision to me. I don't think I could have faced being dropped from the team at that time, for it was a very emotional period and it was then that I really began to miss all the lads. There just seemed an empty space where they had been.

If it wasn't for the crash I am sure we would have developed into one of the great teams of all time, because we had so many great players who, though so young, had already established themselves in top-class football. Duncan Edwards, a full international for England, had not even begun to reach his potential. He had not developed all that much, yet he had managed to reach the top of his profession purely through being a natural player. However, I think Duncan was potentially the greatest player that has ever been seen in British football. He had so much talent and lived for football.

Billy Whelan was another great player we sorely missed in the years to come. He always looked very slow and cumbersome as did Mark Jones, but he was very deceptive. In training he always managed to come first in the mile run.

Jackie Blanchflower was one of our star midfield players and was a sort of understudy to Duncan Edwards. If ever Duncan was unable to play, Jackie would move into this position and always played well. Jackie was very versatile and often took over from Dennis Viollet, playing alongside Tommy Taylor. I really think he was a brilliant player, but his career was shattered before it got off the ground.

The same can be said for Johnny Berry on the wing. He was just developing as a great attacking winger when the crash really put an end to his career. He and Jackie both suffered serious injuries.

Tommy Taylor was one of the most effective players we ever had and was one of the most dominant players I have seen in the air, so much so that we would pass very few balls to his feet. He used to run into a space and be waiting for a high pass which he could take way above the heads of the others. Anyone who let Tommy Taylor run into position was very foolish. I saw him play against one of the best centre halfs in the world, Jesus Garay from Bilbao, and also against Santa Maria of Real Madrid. He murdered them both.

Roger Byrne was our captain and a wonderful man. He was regarded as the 'old man' of the team and was a very different character from any of the other lads. Roger was a very studious type (he was studying to be a physiotherapist) and always thought very hard about what he was doing and what we should be doing. He had a very sharp tongue which he used when the team was not playing well. But I liked him and had a lot of respect for him as a captain.

One person I was particularly sorry to lose in the crash was Bert Whalley, Jimmy's assistant, whom I had known for a very long time, for he was the one who had kept me going in football before I joined United.

Before I became a full-time footballer I worked down the pit for eight years. I was assistant under-manager in a coal mine, earning much more than I did playing for Manchester United. Bert used to write to me every week, keeping me in touch with what was going on at United. I used to train every evening and on Tuesdays and Thursdays, and every weekend, I would come to Manchester to train with the A team. Being a part-time professional and having a job to keep up, I would have to do a full shift down the pit, often starting at 5.30 in the morning and not finishing until 2.30 in the afternoon. I would take a shower at the pithead, grab a bite to eat, and then frequently have to dash for a train to Manchester.

With a life like this I was fitter than many full-time professional footballers.

During this time I was selected to play for England, but I only played the once although I had a good game – perhaps it was because I was only a part-timer. This was a pity, as I needed all the money I was earning as I was saving up to be married. I was earning £11 a week as a footballer and another £15 in the coal mine. I was 21 when I played for England but never played for them again after they found out I was not a full-time professional, though I did play a few times for the Under-23 team.

I was in the United A team when I was 20 and played for them regularly after that. I was never conscious of being a really good footballer and I suppose I was in the team because United did not have anyone really to replace me.

I had been playing right full back for most of my career but did not enjoy it, as I felt this position did not suit me at all. I was not a great tackler and did not like having to go down on the ground in flying tackles. Mark Jones would have made a great full back as he would go into a tackle with all flags flying. It was only after the crash that I really began to enjoy my football because I was then playing centre half.

I was very lucky to have been able to play football for so long; indeed, I played in the European Cup Final when I was 37. I know some players have carried on for longer, and I remember playing in Derek Dougan's testimonial match with Stanley Matthews, who was still playing at 52. I think he certainly looked his age facially, but physically he was still a young man and very fast.

In 1967 I suffered a very serious torn ligament during

a training game and was in splints for several weeks. Even so I was lucky enough to get back into the game to score the goal against Madrid that put us into the final.

Looking back over my time as a footballer, I think I have been very lucky to have played with some of the greatest names in football. For instance, men like George Best, who had a fantastic talent. I don't think anyone in football has been as gifted as Best, which is a shame, because he wasted his talents. I think the best player I ever saw was Dennis Law. I played with him for many years and came to appreciate how good he was. I think Duncan was potentially better but, as we know, he was never given the chance to mature.

Nowadays football is different; a lot has been lost from the game. There is no passion left and the personalities have gone too. All those lads should have been out there scoring the goals.

BILL FOULKES

Born: St Helens, 1 January 1932
League Debut: v Liverpool (Anfield), 13 December 1952
Full International Debut: v Northern Ireland (Belfast),
    22 October 1954

Playing record with Manchester United

Season	Football League		FA Cup		European Cup	
	Games	Goals	Games	Goals	Games	Goals
1952–53	2					
1953–54	32	1	1			
1954–55	41		3			
1955–56	26		1			
1956–57	39		6		8	
1957–58	42		8		8	
1958–59	32		1			
1959–60	42		3			
1960–61	40		3			
1961–62	40		7			
1962–63	41		6			
1963–64	41	1	7			
1964–65	42		7			
1965–66	33		7		8	
1966–67	33	4	1			
1967–68	24	1			6	1
1968–69	10				5	
1969–70	3					
Total	563	7	61		35	1

Playing record with England

1954–55 v Northern Ireland

DENNIS VIOLLET

*'Dennis Viollet was quicksilver, a wonderful
chance-taker. He could read a situation
before a defence could. And not only could
he take chances, he could also create them
with wonderful touches of skill.'*

MATT BUSBY

I still have vivid memories of the Red Star game. Before we went out there, I think we all knew that it was going to be a tremendously difficult task. We had already played Red Star in Manchester and had managed to beat them only 2–1. We knew that they were a very good team with some extremely good players and that we could look forward to a terrific battle. I felt that the team that scored first would probably be the team to win the game. Fortunately for United I managed to score the first goal, which really took the wind out of their sails. This goal was quickly followed by two more from Bob. I think if Red Star had scored first, our task would have been much more difficult.

During the first half of the game we were a very well-composed team, keeping possession of the ball and playing with a great deal of confidence. Just before half-time, I felt a little bit of 'needle' was beginning to creep into the game. Red Star were playing in front of their own crowd and they were 3–0 down – not a position they would have wanted to have been in. Little Sekulorac, the inside forward, started having a go at Duncan Edwards, and Kenny Morgans also ended up with a terrific gash on the front of his leg.

This 'needle' continued increasingly in the second half, when the crowd also started getting at us. Then, when Red Star scored a goal, it was backs to the wall from then on. Even though they were awarded a penalty which they scored from we still felt fairly confident that we could win the game. However, Red Star were awarded a free kick some way outside the penalty area. This was taken by Kostic, their big left winger, who gave the ball an almighty whack. I think the ball would probably have gone over the crossbar but it hit the top of my head, which took a little bit of the pace off it and put some spin on it, deflecting it just under the bar. That made the score 3–3.

All hell was now let loose and we came under tremendous pressure for the rest of the game. Full marks must be awarded to the United team, for they then showed the true character that made them the great team that they have always been. I am sure that had this not been so, on that day we would have lost the game. It was sheer guts and hard work that got us through that match. There were some outstanding performances: I well remember Duncan Edwards displaying an enormous amount of power on the field. Whenever he got the ball it usually took three men to get it away from him. Mark

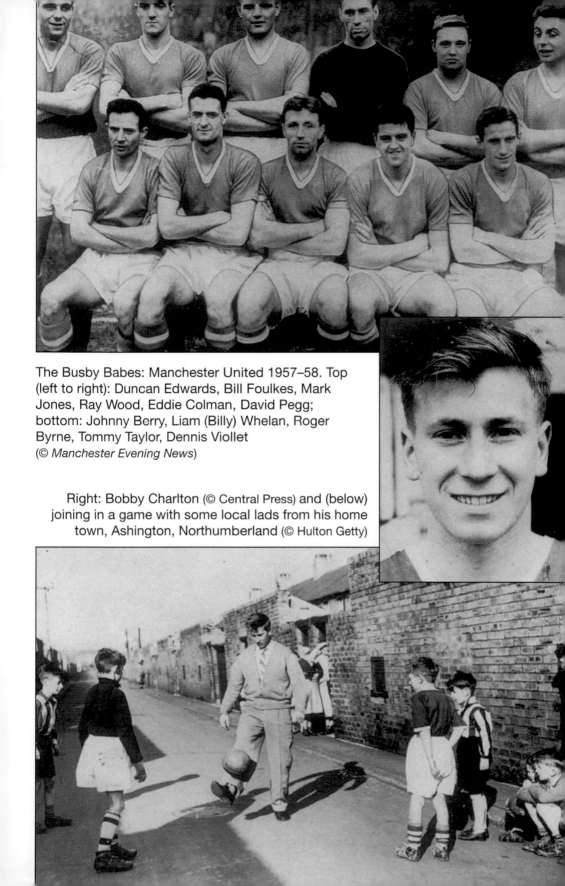

The Busby Babes: Manchester United 1957–58. Top (left to right): Duncan Edwards, Bill Foulkes, Mark Jones, Ray Wood, Eddie Colman, David Pegg; bottom: Johnny Berry, Liam (Billy) Whelan, Roger Byrne, Tommy Taylor, Dennis Viollet
(© *Manchester Evening News*)

Right: Bobby Charlton (© Central Press) and (below) joining in a game with some local lads from his home town, Ashington, Northumberland (© Hulton Getty)

Matt Busby with the team in Jersey (© *Evening Post*, Jersey)

Matt Busby and Jimmy Murphy during the 1958 FA Cup final
against Bolton Wanderers (© Colorsport)

Harry Gregg
(© UPPA)

Ray Wood
(© *Manchester
Evening News*)

Billy Foulkes
(© Express Newspapers)

Kenny Morgans
(© Press Portraits)

Johnny Berry
(© International
Press)

Dennis Viollet
(© Colorsport)

Jackie Blanchflower
(© Express Newspapers)

Left to right: Bobby Charlton, David Pegg and Tommy Taylor
(© *Manchester Evening News*)

Below: Duncan Edwards
(© *Manchester Evening News*)

Right: Albert Scanlon
(© A. Wilkes and Son)

Left: Roger Byrne in action
(© Express Newspapers) and (below)
taking it easy (© PA – Reuters)

Geoff Bent
(© *Manchester Evening News*)

Eddie Colman
(© *Manchester Evening News*)

Mark Jones
(© *Manchester Evening News*)

David Pegg
(© *PA – Reuters*)

1 February 1958. In their final league match before the crash, United beat Arsenal 5–4 at Highbury in what many still regard as one of the finest games ever played in England. Here Taylor and Viollet reach for goal. (© Hulton Getty)

Tommy Taylor
(© News Team
Manchester; inset
© Colorsport)

Liam (Billy) Whelan
(© Colorsport)

Jones, another very powerful player, was unbeatable in the air and really battled it out that day. We owed an awful lot to the speed of Roger Byrne and the great goalkeeping of Harry Gregg. Bill Foulkes took the fight to the Yugoslavs. As I have said, if we had produced anything less we would have gone under. I know that we were all highly delighted and relieved to hear the final whistle, and as we walked off the pitch we gave one another a little hug; we were thrilled to bits.

One of the things that stands out about that match in Belgrade was the huge stadium – thousands and thousands of people shouting and cheering and bombarding us with anything they could get hold of. I remember one or two of the lads giving the crowd the Winston Churchill victory sign. It was an amazingly tough match and it is to the great credit of a wonderful team that we came through it.

After the match there was a banquet at a hotel in Belgrade, attended by both teams. However, the uppermost thought in our minds was not the match we had just played but the next game on Saturday against Wolves. I cannot remember the exact position of either team in the league, but I think that whoever was to win that match would have taken over as leaders of the First Division. We were all fairly elated after the match and the Boss gave us an extra hour or two so that we could have a few beers before going to bed. We were so excited that there was no way any of us could have gone to bed and got to sleep at 11 o'clock. This extension was much appreciated, and I remember going down to the bar and enjoying several beers with Frank Swift. He and I talked for about an hour and a half about the game and I am sure we re-enacted the entire 90 minutes. Then it was off to bed, for we had to be up early in the morning to catch the plane back to Manchester. What a shame it is that one is unable to see the future. Even after we had boarded the plane and there had been two attempts to take off and we had returned to the terminal with 'technical problems', I don't think anybody was particularly worried that we would not get off the ground at the next attempt.

I remember that I was sitting right at the front of the aircraft, facing backwards. Bobby Charlton was sitting next to me and behind me was the journalist Frank Taylor. Across the aisle were Harry Gregg and Bill Foulkes. During the first two attempts to take off, David Pegg was sitting the other side of Bobby Charlton and the three of us were fooling about with Eddie Colman, who was sitting further down the plane. When we reboarded the plane David left us to sit with Eddie Colman, his best friend. If he had stayed where he was in the same row of seats with Bob and me he would probably be with us today.

The plane was one of the old Elizabethans which had wings on top of the fuselage, which meant that those of us sitting underneath the wings could see the wheels. I remember watching them on the final attempt and feeling a terrific surge and then a loss of power as though we were braking. I saw the wheels locking and then once again there was this sensation of a surge and a loss of power. Even then, I don't think anyone was worried; it was just a question of waiting for the plane to leave the ground.

The first thing that made me realise that things were not quite right was the fact that we had come off the end of the runway and were ploughing through a fence and across a road. I turned to Bob and said, 'Hey Bob, just relax.' He too had seen what was happening. Then, in what seemed like a fraction of a second, it was all over. Bob and I, still in our seats, were suddenly 70 yards away from the plane. My head was split and I was covered in blood but Bob seemed to have received only a slight knock to the back of his head. I'd got my head split open.

It is strange what people do in certain circumstances. Bob just got up and walked away. I was not really conscious at the time and didn't quite understand what had happened. I dimly remember walking back to the plane and Bob was there with Bill Foulkes and Harry Gregg. Bob put his arm round me and I asked him the dumbest question of my life: 'Have we crashed, Bob?' It was then I understood what had happened, for I could see the carnage around me.

When I look back on this scene now I see only occasional pictures that flash in my mind as they come and go. But I do remember somehow being put into the back of a Volkswagen van to be taken to the hospital. In the van were Bill Foulkes, who was looking after Matt Busby, and a Yugoslavian lady, both of whom were badly hurt. It was then that we almost suffered a second crash. Bill was asking me whether I was okay and I told him that I was, although I felt I was going to be sick.

Bob, who had also climbed into the van, said he felt the same way. I must have fallen unconscious for a moment because the next thing I remember was the van swerving about at breakneck speed in the snow. I looked up and saw Bill Foulkes with his hands around the driver's neck, trying to strangle him. The van was going all over the place. The driver was anxious to get us to the hospital and was obviously going a bit too fast. Bill felt that somehow he had to stop him. However, things settled down and what would have been a second crash was avoided.

When we got to the hospital all I remember to begin with was seeing Frank Swift lying there just before they began to stitch him up. I think I must have passed out again, for the next memory I have is of waking up in bed in a room with four or five Germans. I think the hospital must have lost me for a few hours in the confusion of people being brought in for emergency treatment. I think that since I was obviously not seriously hurt they had put me to bed in the first vacant room they had found.

It was not until the next day that I was able to think at all clearly and even then my main worry was that my feet and ankles both hurt like hell. Somehow I had lost my shoes in the crash and I think that I had hurt my feet walking about afterwards. But I was very pleased to see that my feet were still there.

Suddenly things started to come back to me and I remembered seeing many of the lads lying on the ground among the debris of the plane. I tried to dismiss this memory from my mind for I was sure that it was not really true, or at the worst that they had, like me, merely been unconscious for a while. Bill Foulkes came to visit me and I asked him about Eddie Colman and whether he was all right. It was then I realised that the pictures flashing through my mind were real and not just a nightmare. It had actually happened. I saw some of the other lads at this stage, for I was put into a room with Kenny Morgans, Bobby Charlton, Jackie Blanchflower and John Berry, although John was shortly moved to another room because of his critical injuries. One of the things that reinstated my sense of reality was hearing Jackie shouting to a nurse to get him a Carlsberg. I remember thinking, 'That sounds like good old Jackie, and she can bring me one too.' There was Jackie with his injuries and all he was bothered about was a bottle of Carlsberg.

I was kept in bed for about a fortnight not being allowed to walk about, even to take a bath or a shower. So I didn't get a chance to see the guys upstairs. They were all together in one room – Johnny, Duncan, Matt, Kenny, Albert, Ray and Bobby, though he was released fairly quickly. When I did eventually manage to get upstairs the first person I saw was Matt. Even then Matt was so ill they had not told him exactly what had happened. His first question to me was 'How are the rest of the boys?' I did not know who had died and I just wished that they were all as well as I, so I could give Matt no news. I never saw Duncan again for although he had been put on a life-support machine and his great strength had kept him going for so long, I was still restricted to bed when he died.

I remember passing the time by playing cards with Jackie Blanchflower until they released me from hospital on condition that I returned every day for treatment. This I did and took the opportunity of seeing Jackie and the other lads. It was good to see them but all I wanted was to get back home. It was not a lot of fun staying in the hotel knowing how everyone in Manchester must be feeling.

Jean Busby and her daughter Sheena were staying at the same hotel. Jean was an absolutely unbelievably amazing woman. She was incredible. I cannot believe how well she faced this disaster, how wonderful she was to all of us and how she comforted us even though Matt was still lying in hospital. I remember one night we were all pretty upset. She and I sat in the bar drinking brandy, which seemed to relax us a little bit – possibly a little bit too much, as we ended up dancing a polka around the bar. This ended in Jean being told that if she didn't behave herself she'd be thrown out. I bet it's the only time Lady Busby had been told that! However, it seemed to relax her and take her mind off things.

While I was visiting the lads in hospital we were able to listen to the match between Manchester United and Sheffield Wednesday. The *Daily Express* had kindly arranged to relay the commentary by telephone to us at the hospital. They did the same for the game against Nottingham Forest a few days later. Hearing these two matches made me feel very homesick and I was determined to get back to Manchester, back to my family, and to start training and get back to full fitness.

I refused to fly back! I took the train from Munich to the Hook of Holland and the boat to Harwich. I remember the morning we arrived back in England. There was a knock on the cabin door and one of the waiters brought me a cup of tea and some biscuits and gave me the wonderful news that Manchester United had beaten West Bromwich the previous evening. Colin Webster had scored the goal, which had been laid on by Bobby Charlton. It was a tremendous welcome home for me.

It was not until I returned to Manchester that I realised what an impact this terrible tragedy had had on everyone. The feeling in the town was unbelievable. A fund had been started for the dependants of the boys who had died and an incredible amount of money had been raised.

Though there was this amazing feeling of sympathy all over Manchester, I felt an awful emptiness. I remember going to Old Trafford but I cannot begin to describe the strange feeling of the place. There was an eerie vacuum and it was difficult to believe what had happened. For me, and I think for many people, Old Trafford could never be the same again. Even though Manchester United has been through great and successful periods since the crash, I don't think they were anything like the team we had beforehand.

There was a particular greatness in Manchester United in that era before the crash and the players had tremendous talent and ability. Wonderful players like Billy Whelan and Tommy now all gone. For me the thing that really made us a great team was the bond, the team spirit that kept us all together. So many of us had grown up together in the United nursery teams. I had been at Old Trafford since I was 16, playing with lads like Roger Byrne and Eddie and David and big Duncan. We were all kids together and had a great relationship. This camaraderie had gone, never to return, and this was the thing I missed more than anything else. It was more than just team spirit. We would have run through a brick wall for United. You could almost say we had a love for one another.

Without that wonderful feeling it was terrible to walk into Old Trafford, but life had to go on and I really wanted to get back into the team. I started training again and although I was warned that any blow on my head could be dangerous, I was very keen to try to make the team as soon as possible.

My first match at Old Trafford was a game against Wolves which we somehow managed to lose 4–0, but it was a game that I thoroughly enjoyed and it was a great feeling to be part of the team once more. However, many of us felt a little guilty because the lads who had battled to get the team through to the FA Cup Final would not be with us. My conscience told me that these were the guys who should be playing and I felt this very strongly. Although I wanted to be fair to the lads, I wanted desperately to play at Wembley, as I had missed playing in the previous year's final against Aston Villa through injury. I spoke to Jimmy Murphy, whom I deeply respected, and said, 'Jimmy would you like me to play again?' Jimmy Murphy said, 'Dennis, that's the best news I've had for a long time. I'd love you to play.' It was through Jimmy that I had the pleasure and honour of playing for United against Bolton Wanderers in the Cup Final at Wembley.

It was a strange feeling; we all wanted to win but we all felt that merely getting to the final was as good as winning it. There was a tremendous amount of emotion and it was this emotion which took us through to Wembley. The objective was to get there; winning the cup would just be icing on the cake. The match will never go down as a classic but I remember enjoying it thoroughly, even though we lost 2–0.

After the match we had a banquet at the Savoy Hotel and the atmosphere there was as though we had won the cup. I am told the atmosphere among the Bolton team was almost as though they had lost.

Some of the doctors who had treated us in Germany had been invited to the banquet and we spent some time chatting to them. I remember the doctor who had warned me about the dangers of playing again was there. She blew me a kiss and wagged her finger at me as though to say, 'You naughty boy!' Some of the families of the lads who died were there and I felt a bit guilty I was there, while their sons or brothers were not.

After the final we had to set about serious training and try to rebuild the team again, and I had a very happy time with United. In the 1959–60 season I had a very successful time and managed to break the United goalscoring record. Shortly after that I was selected to play for England against Hungary and Luxembourg, which seemed to me to be the apex of a footballer's career. After that I contracted a virus and did not play again for the rest of the season.

On my return I played some reserve matches and a testimonial at Stoke City. Stoke City obviously took a shine to me since they did a deal with United and I was transferred to them. I had five very happy years with Stoke and played with some wonderful lads. Harry Gregg came over from Manchester United and made it seem almost like old times.

In 1967 I came to America for the first time and played for the Baltimore Bays for two years. After that I had a happy year playing for Preston North End under Alan Ball. Following that I made a foolish mistake by going as manager to Crewe Alexandra. This just did not work out, which was sad, but it resulted in my coming back to America where I have been ever since, in Baltimore and Jacksonville.

I still think a lot about the old days, and what it meant to be one of the Busby Babes. It was one of the greatest things a guy could wish for. Nothing can compare with the enormous feeling of camaraderie we had. It wasn't just that we looked up to Matt. We looked up to everyone, and they looked up to us. There was always a particular understanding between us, with wonderful men like Jim Murphy and Bert Whalley who did so much for us all. Jim especially had a knack for instilling great enthusiasm in everyone. He did a tremendous job for United and probably never quite got the credit he deserved. Another lovable man who did so much was Walter Crickmer, who could never do enough to help.

Two men who did as much for Manchester as anyone were Bill Inglis, the reserve trainer, and Tom Curry, our father confessor. I remember playing a practical joke on Tom while on tour. We had all gone out for a meal somewhere, and while he wasn't looking we put a rubber cockroach in his chicken salad. God – he jumped a mile! I thought he'd throw it in the head-waiter's face!

Bill was a great comfort. I remember a reserve game against Blackburn in which I had a goal but otherwise played badly. I told Bill I felt I had not done well. 'Look lad,' he said, 'whether you play well or not – a goal covers a multitude of sins!' That always stuck in my mind. After that I felt that if I could score a goal or two it would make up for some of the things I did wrong.

I played for United for 13 years altogether, from my debut at the age of 18 to the day I left for Stoke City in 1962. How well I remember my first game for United. It was against Newcastle and we won by 2–1, Tommy Taylor scoring two great goals. I had some wonderful times. I played in our first ever European Cup game when I scored, beating Anderlecht 2–0 in Brussels. I think I was the first English player to score a goal in the European Cup. That was a great game for us because for some reason the League didn't want us to go into the cup. Another memorable cup game was the return game against Anderlecht in Manchester which we won 10–0 with some of the finest flowing football I've ever seen.

Perhaps the most exciting game was the second leg against Bilbao. They'd beaten us 5–3 in Spain so we had to win the home leg by at least three goals. They were a great team and we knew we had to score early on to be in with a chance. The longer the game went without our scoring, the more Bilbao would be encouraged to hold us off. It wasn't as soon as we would have liked, but after 30 minutes I scored the first goal and that set us going. Shortly afterwards we made it 2–0, to make the aggregate scores even. Then all hell broke loose. I had two goals disallowed for offside, but we kept on and on, battling at their goal. The emotion among the crowd and the players was unbelievable. When Johnny Berry scored that final goal, the whole stadium erupted. From a purist's point of view it wasn't a classic game, but it will be remembered as long as football is played at Old Trafford.

The game I certainly remember is one I didn't play in! That was the FA Cup Final at Wembley against Villa. I had played against West Brom on the previous Wednesday but had strained my groin, so no matter how desperately I wanted to play, I couldn't. I wasn't fit and Bobby Charlton was. But I did make it the following year, after the crash, but it wasn't the same then. I don't think it ever was the same again.

They were all marvellous lads and I have such great memories of them. David Pegg and I used to work the left wing together. He was a very smooth player. It was almost as if he used to glide across the top of the grass, slide past the full back and clip the ball into the net. But he was a very unselfish player. In the match in which we beat Anderlecht 10–0 he was the only forward not to have scored and I had already scored three goals.

Towards the end he could have scored himself but I was in a better position so he pulled it back, giving me my fourth. A great player with a beautiful left-foot shot.

Tommy Taylor and I worked together. In modern terminology we would be the two strikers. What a pleasure it was to play with him. Tommy was the perfect foil for me. Many's the time he would fool the defences into following him, letting the ball run on, leaving a clear path for me. I remember him working down the flank too, as in the Bilbao game when he ran rings round Garay, probably the best centre half in the world. Off he'd go with his beautiful, graceful movement, amazing in such a big bloke. He was wonderful to watch. With all his power he really put their defence under pressure. But whenever I think of Tom, I see him soaring two or three feet above a defender, and then his powerful back would arch and with perfect timing he would head the ball into the back of the net. A great player and a great person to be with as well.

Geoff Bent was really unlucky in a way. With any other club he'd have been in the first team all the time, but our left back was Roger Byrne and he was in a class of his own. But Geoff was a great competitor and as hard as nails. Many's the time I'd seen wingers try to take him on, and that big claw of his left foot would come out and scoop the ball away and off Geoff would go with it. A tremendous competitor and an excellent defender.

What can anyone say about Duncan Edwards that has not already been said many times? Duncan was out of this world, one of the best players I've ever seen, and one of the fittest. There wasn't an ounce of fat on him, and he was so powerful when he ran, his muscles stood out on him. He was so wonderfully talented in so many ways, but to me his outstanding ability was in his ball control.

He could control the ball with any part of his body – head, shoulder, chest, thigh. He was amazing. Duncan was something special.

Billy Whelan was another great player with so much talent. He was a great ball-controller like Duncan, a good passer like Eddie, and a prolific goalscorer. I remember the 1956–57 season Bill scored 33 goals. He was probably one of the best I've ever seen with his back to a defender. He had this little shake and then he'd spin round and he'd be past the defender before he realised what had happened. He was one of the finest gentlemen I've ever met.

Roger Byrne had a terrific match temperament. He was a terrible practice player, quite useless in training and practice games. But put him in a match and he would become a changed man. The bigger the match, the better he played. He was one of the fastest men on the field. If ever anyone tried to pass him he would put on a tremendous burst of speed to get to the ball first.

Mark Jones and I were great friends. We had grown up together and trained together and had played together for England Schoolboys. I think he was probably the best centre half in the First Division. He was enormously strong and had great heading ability. I remember him playing against Nat Lofthouse one day at Old Trafford. Nat must have been sick of the sight of him, for whenever Nat got near the ball there was Mark, taking it away from him, that powerful head sending the ball half the length of the pitch.

Eddie Colman was one of my favourites and never got the praise he deserved. We missed him terribly after the crash. He was a great passer of the ball. He could put the ball alongside you, in front of you, he could clip it over you or curl it round you. He made everyone play and was as strong in defence as in attack. He was a strong tackler and was the ideal 'secret weapon' against Don Revie whenever we played City: Eddie played him so well. A great, great player.

Johnny Berry was a typical Manchester United winger whose job was always to go for the full back. And very good at his job he was too – I've seen him turn so many full backs inside out, passing them to get to the goal. He scored a lot of goals too, for a winger. In the cup match at Bournemouth, when we were having a hard time, being a goal down, Johnny got us out of trouble, getting both our goals. He also scored in our win over Birmingham in the FA Cup semi-finals at Hillsborough. He was a good player, but I think he was unlucky in being around when he was, as there were so many great men around at the same time. We still had Tom Finney then and Stan Matthews was there too at the time, so Johnny found it hard to be really outstanding. But he always tried. Although he was small, two thirds of Johnny was heart; he had the biggest heart I've ever seen, and that's what brought him through. I think that helped him pull through after the crash.

Dennis Viollet died on 6 March 1999.

DENNIS VIOLLET

Born: Manchester, 20 September 1933
League Debut: v Newcastle United (St James' Park),
    11 April 1953
Full International Debut: v Hungary (Budapest),
    22 May 1960

Playing record with Manchester United

Season	Football League		FA Cup		European Cup	
	Games	Goals	Games	Goals	Games	Goals
1952–53	3	1				
1953–54	29	11	1	1		
1954–55	34	20	3	1		
1955–56	34	20	1			
1956–57	27	16	5		6	9
1957–58	22	16	3	3	6	4
1958–59	37	21	1			
1959–60	36	32	3			
1960–61	24	15	1			
1961–62	13	7				
Total	259	159	18	5	12	13

Playing record with England

1959–60 v Hungary
1961–62 v Luxembourg (1)

Goals scored are in brackets.

Also played in the Football League for:

Stoke City, Preston North End

JOHNNY BERRY

*'Johnny was only a small player but he was
all heart. No one had more heart than
Johnny. He was a great footballer.'*

DENNIS VIOLLET

After Johnny Delaney, that remarkable winger of the
1948 cup-winning side, left for Aberdeen, Matt Busby
had no quality player among the emerging Babes to
replace him. His only option was to go to the transfer
market. The great wingers of the time, Stanley Matthews
and Tom Finney, could not be bought for a king's
ransom. The next choice, if choice is the word, was a
young man from Aldershot who was running circles
round some very experienced full backs with Birmingham
City. The Midland side were struggling around the
relegation zone while United were heading for yet
another First Division Championship. When Birmingham
came to Old Trafford it seemed a certainty that United
would collect both points. But what Manchester had not

fully taken into consideration was the 5ft 5in of Johnny Berry. This tough little player picked up the ball in his own penalty area and, beating man after man he ran almost the entire length of the field. As he approached United's penalty area he feigned a pass, accelerated through on his own and hit the ball like a rocket into the back of the net.

United lost that match and Matt did not fancy facing the menace of Berry again. Matt asked Birmingham whether Berry was available for transfer, but Birmingham knew they had a jewel. The following season Johnny came back with Birmingham and once again played havoc with United's defence. Matt persisted with his enquiries to no avail; but later, totally out of the blue, he received a phone call from Birmingham's manager. It was terse and to the point. 'We have agreed to release Johnny Berry, but there can be no quibbling over the figure. We want £25,000 – not a penny less nor a penny more. He's yours if you're willing to pay.'

Matt did not hesitate. He called Jimmy Murphy to his office and in a few minutes they were on the way to Birmingham. Johnny was signed that very day, much to the relief of Matt and the entire Manchester United defence! The price of £25,000, a huge sum in those days, was repaid rapidly by Johnny, who was highly instrumental in United's league championship success in the 1951–52 season.

The diminutive Johnny Berry made up for his lack of size by his enormous courage – the courage to take on experienced and heavy full backs and still beat them. Unlike many wingers of his day, he would also drop back to tackle oncoming forwards. He could hit a ball accurately with tremendous power with either foot and was a winger of the old school, playing inside or outside the full back. There was a variety in his style of play and there were very few full backs who had a happy match against him.

His experience and his level head saved United in the cup tie against Bournemouth when they were down to ten men, having lost Mark Jones in the 11th minute. Bournemouth scored first and gained in confidence every moment thereafter; but Johnny was once again the bane of the defence, scoring twice that day, once from the penalty spot.

His finest goal was probably against Bilbao in the European Cup when Bilbao came to Maine Road with a 5–3 lead. The atmosphere that night was electrifying, with the ground packed to capacity hours before the kick-off. By half-time United had scored only once, through Dennis Viollet, and desperately needed at least two more goals in order to get through. After 70 minutes Tommy Taylor crashed in the second goal. The crowd were screaming for a third, but no matter how hard they shouted nor how much United tried, nothing seemed to go right. A draw seemed certain with only five minutes to go.

Suddenly the remarkable relationship that had developed between Tommy Taylor and Johnny emerged, showing what intuitive football is all about. Tommy eluded the mighty Garay by moving off to the right with the ball. Johnny, sensing what his colleague was up to, held back until a space had been created in the middle. Tommy cut in towards the goal to angle a shot and, with 60,000 hysterical fans urging them on, he changed direction, calmly stroking the ball to where he instinctively knew Johnny was waiting. Unhesitatingly,

Johnny smashed it into the net for one of the greatest goals in one of the finest victories in the history of the club.

Johnny went on to score many goals for United but three months before Munich, when he was 30, he lost his place to the 18-year-old Kenny Morgans through loss of form. Kenny received only support from Johnny during this period.

Despite losing his place, Johnny went to Belgrade as a reserve and thus became a casualty at Munich. The severity of his injuries prevented him from playing ever again. He returned to his home in Aldershot and for many years afterwards ran a sports shop with his brother.

The history of Manchester United is one full of tales and courage – the courage to carry on irrespective of the pain or the emptiness. Johnny Berry will rate highly in that history, not only for the courage he showed as a player but for the courage he showed after the crash.

Johnny Berry died on 23 September 1994.

JOHNNY BERRY

Born: Aldershot, 1 June 1926
Died: 16 September 1994
League Debut: (for United) v Bolton Wanderers
 (Burnden Park), 1 September 1951
Full International Debut: v Argentina (Buenos Aires),
 17 May 1953

Playing record with Manchester United

Season	Football League		FA Cup		European Cup	
	Games	Goals	Games	Goals	Games	Goals
1951–52	36	6	1			
1952–53	40	7	4			
1953–54	37	5	1			
1954–55	40	3	3			
1955–56	34	4	1			
1956–57	40	8	5	3	8	2
1957–58	20	4			3	1
Total	247	37	15	3	11	3

Playing record with England

1952–53 v Argentina, Chile, Uruguay
1955–56 v Sweden

Also played in the Football League for:

Birmingham City

ALBERT SCANLON

'Albert was unbelievable. He was a great attacking goalscoring winger who could use either foot. He could run past people as if they were standing still.'

BILL FOULKES

'Scanny was very dangerous, a very unpredictable player and, like all wingers at Old Trafford, gave full backs nightmares.'

DENNIS VIOLLET

I remember before I came to United I was at St Wilfred's School at Hulme, where football was my passion. I used to score over 100 goals a year for the team. One day someone came to me and asked if I was Scanlon and whether I had a birth certificate. I replied yes I was and no I didn't. So he took me to All Saints, who furnished me with the birth certificate. It turned out that he was Ted Webb, a sports teacher at St Margaret's, which was Dennis Viollet's school. He told me to turn up at the

Victoria Monument the following Wednesday, when I would be playing for Manchester Schools against Bolton in the Lancashire Cup. That was my first big game.

After that I played fairly regularly for the school's team at Newton Heath Loco, which was a bit like playing at Wembley for us. After one of these matches I saw Ted Webb again and he asked me if I would like to play for Manchester United. I was 14 at the time. I said, 'Yeah, I'd love to play for United.' He said, 'Right.' I never saw him again! So I thought, 'That's it. I won't make United.'

After I had left school, when I was 16, my dad told me one day that I had to go to Old Trafford the following Sunday to meet Mr Busby. I put on my best grey suit and my purple school cap and went over to Old Trafford and walked into the dressing-room. I introduced myself to Bill Inglis and told him that Mr Busby wanted to see me. He told me to sit on the bench and wait. I was so small that my feet wouldn't touch the ground. Soon a man walked in and Inglis said to him, 'This must be one of yours, Boss, his bloody feet don't touch the ground.' I never said a word. Inglis asked me if I was going to sign for United and I told him that I had been promised the chance. Matt Busby told me to return the following morning to sign on and that I could then start work there. I told Mr Busby that I wanted to be a plumber and he said if that was the case they would get me a job as a plumber. However, after I had signed on as an amateur, that notion went straight out of my head.

I remember that the first time I played for United, Bert Whalley came to me and told me to be at the Queens Ground the following Saturday where the juniors and the colts used to meet. In those days the professionals (the A

88

team) used to meet at the Grand Hotel around the corner. I remember that first game vividly. The most memorable part of it all was the smell. We were playing at Barnsley and the ground was next door to a pig farm. There were 20 people at that match! Shortly afterwards Les Olive told me to report to the club where I was to play centre forward for the B team. It was then that I met David Pegg, whom I had played against when he was inside left for Yorkshire Schools. He was a lot bigger than me and when he joined United he went straight into the A team, whereas I played for the juniors.

After that I was off the game for six months with what Jimmy Murphy called growing pains. That first year was nearly a disaster for me as there were so many young lads coming into the team and I was unable to play. However, the following year I started playing with the B team and one day Bert Whalley phoned and told me that they were starting a youth team and had drawn Leeds in the first round; I was to join this team and we were to train on Tuesday nights. This was a good sign for me because it was reckoned that those who played on a Tuesday night were close to being in the A team. The first time I played on a Tuesday, Bert Whalley said to me, 'You've cracked it, Albert; you had the full back (Billy Foulkes) in two minds. He didn't know whether to kick you over the stands or into the dressing-room.' I was still pretty small.

I was promoted and made 12th man for a match against Barnsley, where I saw Tommy Taylor for the first time. Ten minutes into the match Jimmy Murphy kept saying to his scout:, 'Look at the centre forward, look at the centre forward.' A week later they signed Tommy for Manchester United – proof of Jimmy's foresight. After that I became a regular in the A team, but I was still learning.

I made my debut against Arsenal in November 1954 and played quite well. In my second league match against West Bromwich, when we were 2–0 down, Johnny Berry centred a ball and I jumped and nodded it hard but it hit the post and came out. Suddenly somebody clouted me round the ear and I turned to see that it was our centre half Allenby Chilton. 'Not like that,' he said. 'You have to head it down – like this.' He showed me how and then ran off to get on with the game. I never made that mistake again. And to think we were losing the match and he still had time to belt me. That's what United were all about.

In order to break the monotony of training we would play hide and seek until the last one was found. We usually did this if it was foggy. We'd scatter absolutely anywhere about the ground. I remember finding Allenby Chilton up a flag pole once and Reg Allen under a wheelbarrow. I'd only just joined the club then and it struck me as odd that great players like Jack Rowley and Stan Pearson were out looking for me while I was trying to conceal myself in the lavatory. It was a great leveller, that game. It really created a marvellous spirit throughout the club.

While this spirit was being developed, the competition for places still went on. Dear Bill Inglis used to wander round with his Woodbine in his hand while we were lapping or doing some exercises. Then he would sidle up to me and in a rasping, confidential whisper used to say, 'Albert – that David Pegg – you could get his place, you know. I tell you Albert, he's not fit to lace your boots. You keep at it son, you'll get his place.' He was building my confidence all the time. Then he'd go slowly across to David and say, 'You'd better watch it Dave, Albert's been telling me he's after your place – he's good you know.' That was his way of geeing us all up, keeping us on our toes.

Being a regular member of the team I was selected to play in the Red Star match. I don't remember much about Belgrade apart from the fact that it was very cold and that we drew the match. Afterwards I remember being invited to the American Embassy where I was given a bottle of gin, which I took back to the hotel. I recall after we had landed in Munich to refuel that there had been a couple of attempts to take off, and the second time I think we had almost made it but then we had to go back to the terminal while some technical problem was sorted out.

When we got back into the plane, various card schools started up among the players. Earlier I had been sitting with Kenny Morgans, Billy Foulkes, and David Pegg, but we had split up as David no longer wanted to play. He went to the back of the plane with Tommy and Eddie. There was another card school with Geoff Bent, Jackie Blanchflower, Johnny Berry, Ray Wood, Roger Byrne and Billy Whelan; and on the other side of the aisle were Billy Foulkes, Kenny Morgans, David Pegg and me. I remember Bobby Charlton and Dennis Viollet, who had earlier been sitting at the back, came forward to the front of the plane. Eddie and David moved to seats at the back. Matt Busby was sitting behind me and the journalists were behind him. There were only players at the front of the plane. The steward who had been sitting across the aisle from me got up to go to the back of the plane where he shut the door prior to take-off.

During the final attempt to take off it became obvious that we weren't going to make it and Billy Whelan looked at me and said, 'Albert, this is the end but I'm ready for it.' I remember nothing after that until I woke in the hospital and somehow I had a telephone in one hand and with the other was holding a nurse's hand. I remember I was shouting something down the telephone. I remember looking round and discovering I was in a room with the co-pilot, Dennis Viollet and Ray Wood, with Bobby Charlton and Kenny Morgans at the other end. Soon after that I either fell asleep or lost consciousness. I woke up to hear a voice saying 'Albert Scanlon will never play football again'.

Just then Jimmy Murphy walked in and came to the end of my bed. I was crying and told him what I had heard. He said, 'That's not true, Albert, you're all right. The doctors say you will be playing again soon. Take my word for it.' That was enough for me, since it came from Jimmy.

I also remember Sister Almunder, who was one of the nurses who looked after me. She came in with one of the doctors, who said to me, 'Ah, Mr Scanlon, it's nice to see you awake. It's the first time I've seen you conscious in the six days you've been here.'

We began to receive visitors at this time. There were some Irish girls from a nearby village who brought us cases of cigarettes and drink – a present from the American forces stationed there. Some of the families started to come over as well, but I was confined to my bed and was not allowed to see the other lads. Eventually I was allowed to use a wheelchair and Sister Almunder used to wheel me about the hospital. I remember having a wheelchair race with Ray Wood one day to see who could get to the church first! Sister Almunder wheeled me round to see the other lads but some of them, like Johnny Berry, were too ill. I was taken to see Jackie Blanchflower but he was too poorly to chat. I also saw the Boss, who was in a mess. It was then that I began to realise exactly what had happened.

Jean Busby came to see us twice a day and would laugh and joke with us as though nothing had happened. She was wonderful and took our minds off the tragedy we were going through, though all the time she must have been frantically worried about Matt, who was lying in an oxygen tent, his legs broken, his body full of tubes. She was genuinely concerned about how we were. Eventually all my injuries were treated and I was allowed to leave hospital and return to Manchester.

Since that time I have often, out of curiosity, sat down late at night and put together on paper my ideal football team for Manchester United and England. My friends who perished in the plane figure strongly in all my teams.

One who figures in every team is Mark Jones. There have been very few players like Mark; the only one who springs to mind is big Jack Charlton. I remember a particular story about Mark. We were due to leave Old Trafford at 7 a.m. for an important match and at 7.30 he had still not arrived. Eventually we could wait no longer and started slowly to drive down the road. At last, at 8.30, he arrived in his brown overcoat, his Frank Sinatra hat and his pipe. Tom Curry ran out shouting, 'Where the hell have you been?' And the Boss had a go at him too. 'You should have gone without me,' said Mark. Tom Curry asked him what the problem had been and Mark said, 'One of my budgies was ill and I'll not leave one of them for anything.' He was as gentle as a mouse off the field, but on it he was as hard as nails.

Another man who has played in every team I have ever thought of was Duncan Edwards. I once asked Jimmy Murphy who was the greatest footballer he had ever seen. He said to me, 'Albert, you were a very good player, you know, if you weren't you'd never have worn that shirt; but I've seen them all and Duncan Edwards must be the greatest of them all.' I can't argue with a man like Jimmy.

Off the field Duncan was slow and cumbersome and gave the impression that he was disinterested in everything around him; but give him a ball and it was as though a whole new horizon opened up before him, because what he did with it was like magic. I once saw him in a European Cup match run all the way down the field from the half-way line, with players coming at him from all sides, and there he was bouncing the ball on his head as though he was just at a practice match! That man was magic.

The man I admired most at United was Roger Byrne, our captain. I had always been a little afraid of Johnny Carey, the previous captain, because of his fame and his status. When I first met Johnny Carey he had been made 'Footballer of the Year' and I remember never speaking to him unless he spoke to me first. I felt it was not my place to do so. It was quite different with dear old Roger. Although he was just as much a gentleman as Johnny Carey, we always felt that Roger understood us as well as he understood football. One of the things that I think is wrong with football today is that there does not seem to be discipline and respect commanded by men like Roger.

Geoff Bent was a little like Mark in one way: off the

field he was very quiet, but in a game of football he assumed a particular personal dynamism. I remember always thinking that his arms seemed longer than his body.

Tommy Taylor, who was afraid of nobody on or off the pitch, was yet another dynamic and energetic player. When he was playing, you didn't have to bother looking for the ball, you merely looked for Tommy – he was never far away from it. When he had the ball there were few who could stand in his way.

Billy Whelan never knew quite how good he was. Although he had won championship and FA Cup medals, he did not seem to realise, or if he did he was embarrassed by, his own skills. He was generally a slow player but despite this played with cunning. He had amazing ball control and having beaten you twice could, just to be cheeky, come back and beat you again.

Johnny Berry was only a little fellow, but on his day he could be compared with Stanley Matthews. He had a wonderful shot and could kick the ball left- or right-footed with equal strength.

I don't think I played my best for United until after Munich and perhaps my best game for them was against West Ham some time later. But in 1960 things began to go wrong for me and I was frequently dropped from the team. I was not told why and I didn't ask and in November 1960 I moved to Newcastle.

Looking back over my time with United I remember so many happy days and so many happy friends. They were the players I grew up with, they were part of my family. I miss them still.

ALBERT SCANLON

Born: Manchester, 10 October 1935
League Debut: v Arsenal (Highbury), 20 November
 1954

Playing record with Manchester United

Season	Football League		FA Cup		European Cup	
	Games	Goals	Games	Goals	Games	Goals
1954–55	14	4				
1955–56	6	1				
1956–57	5	2				
1957–58	9	3	2		3	
1958–59	42	16	1			
1959–60	31	7	3	2		
1960–61	8	1				
Total	115	34	6	2	3	

Also played in the Football League for:

Newcastle United, Lincoln City, Mansfield Town

RAY WOOD

*'He had lightning reflexes and made many
world-class saves. It surprised me he only
ever got three caps for England.'*

DENNIS VIOLLET

*'You didn't get miracles from Ray.
He was just there when it mattered.'*

MATT BUSBY

I played for Newcastle as an amateur before signing for
Darlington in 1949. Just a few months later I was
transferred to Manchester United for £6,000 and was
there throughout the remarkable transition period, from
Johnny Carey's famous side up to the great pre-Munich
days. I stayed at United for exactly nine years, joining
them on 4 December 1949 and being transferred on 4
December 1958 to Huddersfield where I stayed for six
years.

During my time at Huddersfield, United tried to buy
me back when Harry Gregg injured his shoulder but

97

Huddersfield did not tell me. Matt told me he had been trying for six weeks to get me back and the Huddersfield management told me later that they could not have released me as they had no one to replace me. I would have loved to have gone back to United but that's the luck of the draw. I had a good innings and was a professional goalkeeper for 20 years.

I remember that when I was called for my National Service I was afraid that it would interrupt my career, but after a few weeks of square bashing I was called to the Station Commander and told that United were desperate for a goalkeeper and wanted me. He said, 'I hope this isn't going to happen very often, Wood.' I replied, 'No Sir, only every weekend!' Either he must have appreciated my cheek or United sent him tickets, for I was allowed to play for them regularly after that.

In the early '50s I played against some remarkable sides like Arsenal, Spurs and Portsmouth who were a tremendous team. I was up against top-class centre forwards like Dougie Reid, Jackie Milburn, John Charles and Trevor Ford. Each team seemed to have such strength of character in those days and men of that calibre really made their mark upon the game. I played my first game for United with those two great international full backs, gentleman Johnny Carey and John Aston. 'What a start,' I thought. 'I could never play for a better team.' Little did I realise then that United would emerge to be an even greater side.

I played throughout the '50s with the Babes and was honoured to be chosen to play for England on three occasions. I was the England reserve goalkeeper six times too. During that period I won two First Division Championship medals with United. My first international match was against Ireland when Bill Foulkes also made his international debut. I gather we both played well. I remember Stanley Matthews was in the team then; he was getting on at this time and always had a sleep before a game, but what energy he had. He could outrun men half his age.

One man Matthews could never outrun was Roger Byrne. He was a really good back and would anticipate the play and get in as soon as the other player had got the ball. Roger was never a hard tackler but did not need to be, as he was so skilful. Even he was not the fastest in the team, however; that honour fell to me!

United had been pretty successful up till the game in Belgrade. I knew I was only going as Harry's deputy but it promised to be a good game, and so it proved. I remember landing at Munich on the return flight and we all got off the plane in order to go for coffee. When we tried to take off for the second time a lot of us got rather nervous and when that take-off was aborted and we went back to the terminal to await our call, we were even more nervous. I think if someone had suggested that we go back by train and boat we would all have agreed, but no one thought of this so we went back to the aircraft.

I remember that Roger was sitting in front of me with a camera when we took off but I remember nothing else until I woke up and found myself half in and half out of the plane with the wheels on top of me. I have no idea how I got into that position. I think I must have been very close to the point at which the aircraft split in half. Some men appeared with a crowbar and began to lever the wheels away so that they could get me out. Unfortunately, in their anxiety to get me free they were levering my leg as well and broke it! I must have been unconscious for some time before this as Harry had seen me and thought I was dead. When I came to, the first thing I did was ask Peter Howard of the *Daily Mail* for a cigarette. He gave me one and was about to light it when somebody stopped him, pointing out that we were underneath the ruptured petrol tanks.

After I had been moved to the hospital I realised that apart from my broken leg I had split my lip and the inside of my eyelid. The doctors thought I might lose the sight of my eye. It was covered for weeks but the doctors were very clever and I have had no ill-effects since, although I still suffer from occasional headaches.

Even amidst all the anguish in the hospital there was, in retrospect, some humour. The doctors had X-rayed my leg and told me that they would use a steel plate in a plaster cast to support the break. Two days later I was still in great pain and complained to the professor that his famous treatment was not doing me any good. Upon checking he discovered, to his chagrin, that the Yugoslav in the next bed had my steel plate on his perfectly healthy leg!

I am an obsessive tea-drinker and like my tea strong and hot. I remember asking one of the nurses for some tea as soon as I arrived at the hospital and she brought me some cold peppermint tea in a feeding bowl! I was lying there drinking cold tea worrying about my leg, which by then was also very cold, and thinking about the film *All Quiet on the Western Front*, where people were smiling at the patients and making a point of not telling them about their amputated legs. But mine were still there.

I was worried about my wife and whether she now knew that I was all right. I learned later that she had received the news in a bizarre and upsetting way. She had been hanging out the washing in the garden when the lady next door came out and said, 'Mrs Wood, does Ray know the plane has crashed and most of them are dead?' She obviously thought that as Harry was the goalkeeper I would still be in Manchester. Fortunately, the news got through later that I was comparatively healthy.

I was in hospital for several days, not knowing who had survived and who had not. People kept reassuring me that some of my friends were in other hospitals and that was why I could not see them. It was not until I came out of hospital that I realised the extent of the tragedy.

Apart from my other injuries, I must have taken quite a knock on the head, for all the time I had a terrific screaming noise in my ears and even asked people to turn off the radio, even though there wasn't one on. I began to develop double vision and every time the nurse put out two tablets for me to take I could see four and kept picking up fresh air. It was like something out of Laurel and Hardy. When I got out of hospital in Munich I was sent back to Manchester, but had to spend some time in St Joseph's Hospital where, for some reason, they took out all my teeth. Dennis Viollet found out about this and brought me an apple. Typical of Dennis!

When I was fit enough to return to football I was given one game in the reserves against Derby but, needless to say, I played a stinker. All my confidence had gone. I had many nightmares after the crash and would often wake up still talking to the lads. They were, after all, a marvellous bunch and I was not going to forget them in a hurry.

It was not long before I was fully fit and able to play well again, but only months later I was bought by Huddersfield.

There is one story I always remember of those days at

United which still makes me smile. Dennis, Mark, Geoff Whitefoot and I used to do the pools. One Saturday we were checking the results and realised that we had won a second dividend. We were all over the moon and told everyone to expect some millionaires in the club! Dennis worked in town and we arranged for him to get the paper early on Tuesday morning and to phone us to let us know the extent of our fortunes. We were to start our lifetime celebrations with a slap-up meal at the Midland Hotel that night and hardly slept on Monday night. We arrived early at the ground to await Dennis's call. The phone rang and Dennis told us the wonderful news. We had won £28! Later Matt called us over from training and told us, with a smile on his face, that the man from Littlewoods had come to present us with our cheque. It was back to pie and Bovril days again!

Ray Wood died on 7 July 2002.

RAY WOOD

Born: Hebburn, 11 June 1931
League Debut: (for United) v Newcastle United
(Old Trafford), 3 December 1949
Full International Debut: v Northern Ireland
(Belfast), 2 October 1954

Playing record with Manchester United

Season	Football League		FA Cup		European Cup	
	Games	Goals	Games	Goals	Games	Goals
1949–50	1					
1950–51						
1951–52						
1952–53	12		4			
1953–54	27		1			
1954–55	37		3			
1955–56	41		1			
1956–57	39		6		8	
1957–58	20				4	
1958–59	1					
Total	178		15		12	

Playing record with England

1954–55 v Northern Ireland, Wales
1955–56 v Finland

Also played in the Football League for:

Darlington, Bradford City, Huddersfield Town, Barnsley

JACKIE BLANCHFLOWER

*'It was a magnificent feeling to know
you had a guy like Jackie. He did a
tremendous job for us.'*

DENNIS VIOLLET

I first came to United in March 1949 having been spotted
in Ireland by a local scout who obviously put in a good
word for me. I always wanted to be a professional
footballer. My brother Danny used to say that when he
got to England and started playing football he would
send for me. Ironically, although he is seven years older
than me, I was there before him.

There I was, a 16-year-old lost Irish boy standing at the
station in Manchester, when Matt Busby himself came to
meet me.

The ground at Manchester was nothing like as large as
it is today, for when I arrived there were only a couple of
stands. For a long time we did little odd jobs, cleaning the
boots and calling all the senior players 'mister'. We
trained only in the morning and were taken under the

wings of the more experienced men. Johnny Carey and Jimmy Delaney in particular looked after me. On Tuesday and Thursday evenings, Jimmy Murphy and Bert Whalley took us youngsters to train on our own. There was lots of trapping, turning, heading, twisting and ironing-out of faults. We played plenty of five-a-side games as well.

When I was 17, I was offered professional terms which I accepted and was paid a £10 signing-on fee, which I gave to my mother. In 1951 I was playing in the Central League with Roger and Mark and in November of that year Roger and I played our first game for United in the first team against Liverpool at Anfield. The press gave us both a good write-up for that match. I also got a cut eye in that match and needed five stitches, leaving me with a permanent scar. Unfortunately while I was training on my own later that week I tore a knee ligament and did not play again for nine months; when I was finally fit again we went on tour to America. I remember when we were in Hollywood we met some of the British actors. We also met Edmond Glenn, Victor McGlaglan and Bob Hope, who were all very friendly.

Tom Curry was our trainer. He was an uncanny genius whose death was a great loss to the club. He would treat each one of us as his son. He would build up our confidence and each of us would think that what Tom was saying was unique to us, though he would be saying the same to everyone else. He really kept us fit. Tom has a theory that a racehorse should be trained to be fit for the day of the race, not like other trainers who trained them to be fit for the day before.

Our training started five weeks before the beginning of the season; from about 12 July we would train for about two hours in the morning and two hours in the afternoon. For the first two weeks we'd be as stiff as boards. We trained at the university ground, running lap after lap of the track. After two weeks, when we were fit, we would be given a ball for the first time. The emphasis was placed on fitness so that we had a really sound basis for the rest of the season.

In the practice games there was plenty of needle between us as each of us was playing for a place in the team; no one was ever certain of his place. The club always promoted this competitiveness, Tom or Matt sometimes stopping the match to discuss particular points. There was a lot of one-upmanship, but never any animosity.

Training could sometimes be a grind, so to break the monotony Tom would get us to play hide and seek. I remember one particular day when England were playing a Test against Australia at the Old Trafford cricket ground, and we had been unable to find Colin Webster. It was not until two days later when he blurted out the Test score that we knew where he had been!

The only day we did not train was Monday, when we played golf virtually all day. I played with a handicap of four. This was all part of the club's idea of keeping the players together, keeping the 'family' intact. Matt was a golfing fanatic, and he enjoyed our Monday sessions, but he was very much the 'Boss'. We still had, amongst us youngsters, some of the older players – men like Johnny Carey, Jack Rowley, Stan Pearson and Charlie Mitten. We were very much a team and I was sorry when Charlie Mitten left us for Bogota. On his return, even though he had left the 'family', Matt let him train at the ground. Charlie was a great player and very underrated. I once saw him score three penalties against Aston Villa. After he left us he had some good years with Fulham; he was a very gifted player.

Matt's only thoughts were to build up the best team possible and I remember the groundsman complaining to him once that the players were messing up his pitch. Matt said to him, 'Do you want the best team and the worst pitch or the worst team and the best pitch?' He never complained again. We certainly had the best team. We were doing so well that season and had beaten Red Star in Manchester, so we only had to draw in Belgrade.

I remember how cold it was out there. My main impression of Yugoslavia was of its bleakness and of people queuing. It was my first trip to the Eastern Bloc and I am afraid it didn't make a very good impression on me. I don't remember much about the game, apart from the last few moments which were very tense. After the match there was a banquet at which Red Star made us a present of some coffee cups. We left the next morning for Munich, where we refuelled. We tried to take off twice without success and I remember Alf Clarke phoning home to say we might have to stay in Munich overnight – but we tried a third take-off. It was like going down a cobbled road.

After the crash, I was thrown clear of the aircraft. I was conscious and aware of what was going on; my mind was still active. I remember seeing the fire where the aircraft hit the house, and seeing Bobby Charlton wandering about. I saw Harry and Bill Foulkes going in and out of the plane, helping people to get clear.

I was quite badly injured and bleeding a lot. Harry came over to me and tied my arm in a tourniquet and I think this might have saved my arm. I was piled into a van with Johnny Berry and taken to the hospital. I must have been in a bad way because I was given the Last Rites. I am thankful for Tom Curry's fitness training, for I'm sure I'd never have survived had I not been so fit.

At the time I thought that it was only poor Roger who had died. I was put in a room with one of the pilots and Johnny Berry and later moved into another room with Duncan, who was very ill. Later I was moved yet again into a room with a German who had a German newspaper, and it was only then that I learnt the true extent of the catastrophe. My final move was into a room with Frank Taylor and I remember every time I tried to get some sleep, he was on the phone to his paper in Manchester. I was in there for 13 weeks!

When I got home I was still in a bad way. My pelvis had been smashed and I had broken my arm and 13 ribs and damaged my kidneys. Most of my injuries recovered slowly to a great extent but I had to have my arm in plaster for 18 months. The Germans, who are a truthful race, told me that my arm would be 'kaput', but it turned out not too bad. I returned to Manchester on the Saturday of the FA Cup semi-final, but I didn't go to that match or the final as I could not stand being jostled in the crowd.

Munich was one of those things that sometimes happens; it was tragic but you have to carry on and maintain your sense of humour. Although Munich saw the end of my footballing career I have had a good life. I had some good years with United and played 13 times for Ireland. My brother, Danny, played over 60 times for his country and I am sure that had things turned out differently I would have done the same.

Jackie Blanchflower died on 2 September 1998.

JACKIE BLANCHFLOWER

Born: Belfast, 7 March 1933
League Debut: v Liverpool (Anfield), 24 November
   1951
Full International Debut: v Wales (Wrexham), 31 March
   1954

Playing record with Manchester United

Season	Football League		FA Cup		European Cup	
	Games	Goals	Games	Goals	Games	Goals
1951–52	1					
1952–53	1					
1953–54	27	13	1			
1954–55	29	10	3			
1955–56	18	3				
1956–57	11		2		3	
1957–58	18				2	
Total	105	26	6		5	

Playing record with Northern Ireland

1953–54 v Wales
1954–55 v England, Scotland
1955–56 v Scotland (1), Wales
1956–57 v England, Scotland, Portugal
1957–58 v Scotland, England, Italy

Goals scored are in brackets.

KENNY MORGANS

*'The thing I'll always remember about Kenny
is what great confidence he had.'*

DENNIS VIOLLET

I played first for the Swansea Schoolboys and then later for the Welsh Schoolboys. I played for Wales against England at Maine Road and I was spotted by Jimmy Murphy and Bert Whalley. I had a good game and they were impressed and came down to Swansea to sign me up. I was 15 at the time.

United really looked after me and I stayed with Mrs Evans, who worked at United. I stayed with her for two years before I signed professional forms at 17. Bert and Jimmy really worked hard on me to improve my game. Jimmy shortened my running pace because I used a long stride when I ran and this sometimes put me off balance. In December 1957 Johnny Berry wasn't playing very well so I got in at outside right against Leicester City and we won 3–1. I was only 18 then. The crowd on that day was so large – but I'd had a good apprenticeship in the youth

111

team through to the reserves. In those days the youth team won the FA Youth Cup five times. I became captain of the youth team just before my first game in the senior team.

Jimmy Murphy was a great help because he was also manager of Wales. His team talks were an inspiration. However, when I played for the Welsh Under-23 team he sent me out of the room from the team because he thought I'd probably heard it too many times and I'd laugh! When he knew I was up against a really good full back he'd come and sit next to me and say, 'This full back's got a good left foot, a good right foot, he can run like a gazelle, he's fantastic in the air, he's unbeatable, but he's nothing. You go out and play him off the field!'

I played three months in the first team before Munich and I was not on the losing side once. Johnny Berry was in the reserves then and although he must have felt it, he was professional enough to accept it. There were a number of excellent reserves all knocking at the door of the first team – and they were all good. Geoff Whitefoot was always shouting at me when I made mistakes, but when I did well he'd come and put his hand on me.

After Munich everything changed because there were players in the team that would never have made the first team under normal circumstances. I think I started back too early. It was only six weeks after the crash. I came home on the Thursday and on the Saturday I was playing in the reserves. I had two games with them and then straight into the first team. It was all different; we had Stan Crowther and Ernie Taylor. I had played in most of the games up to the Cup Final, so I was expecting to play. But on the day before Jimmy thought the atmosphere would be too much for me so he said he was going to play Dennis instead. So Dennis came in at inside right and Webster took my place. I was very disappointed, very disappointed. I stayed for a couple more seasons and then went to Swansea. I played for three seasons and packed it in to run a pub for ten years. Bill Lucas got me out of retirement to play for Newport County in the Fourth Division. It really wasn't easy for me but I enjoyed it.

I think that the Arsenal match prior to the Belgrade game was a fantastic game. People say it was one of the finest games ever seen at Highbury. But of course the match with Red Star was a great game. They had a goalkeeper they called the 'Black Cat' who said no one could beat him from outside the box. He was so confident, but of course Bobby took the smile off his face with his mighty drive from outside the area. I played well up until half-time and then as we kicked off I saw their full back coming towards me. I wasn't sure if he was going to kiss me or shake my hand. He didn't do either, he just kicked me in the thigh – I was off for 20 minutes and the referee didn't see anything happen so he got away with it!

The only thing I remember about the crash was the Boss saying beforehand that he wanted us to get back home on the Thursday so that we could have one good day's rest before playing Wolves on the Saturday. The only thing I did on that Saturday was to wake up for the first time in 48 hours. At my bedside were two German reporters. The professor told me who had lived and who had died. The reporters told me that they had been to the crash scene and that I was the last to come out. I'd been in a deep coma for two days and I'd had a lot of blood given to me. The nuns and doctors were so marvellous. I remember Duncan's 21st birthday in that hospital.

I watch football on the box and I realise that I had the honour of playing for the greatest team of all time. They were immortals – just think of Eddie Colman. He was fantastic; it was like having another inside forward with you. And what a powerhouse that half-back line was. But then they were all great; every single member of that team could put the ball on a sixpence. We are never going to see their like again.

KENNY MORGANS

Born: Swansea, 16 March 1939
League Debut: v Leicester City (Old Trafford),
    21 December 1957

Playing record with Manchester United

Season	Football League		FA Cup		European Cup	
	Games	*Goals*	*Games*	*Goals*	*Games*	*Goals*
1957–58	13		2		4	
1958–59	2					
Total	15		2		4	

Also played in the Football League for:

Swansea Town, Newport County

BOBBY CHARLTON

*'You could be under the collar, going through
a bad time and suddenly Bobby would get
the ball, drop his shoulder, go past
somebody and let go one of his tremendous
shots, bang into the back of the net. It'd give
you that bit of confidence and you'd go on
and win games just because of it.'*

DENNIS VIOLLET

I went straight from school in a small north-east mining village to Old Trafford and so Manchester was a bit forbidding. Joe Armstrong, who first spotted me playing, brought me over. Getting into the club initially was difficult because in those days you couldn't sign on as an apprentice. You had to take a job. So I took one with an electrical engineers in Altrincham until I was 17, when I could sign on as a professional. This really used to drive me mad because some of the other younger players had gone on to the ground staff at Old Trafford. All they did was to work on the ground, but they were involved with the players and I wasn't. This was very frustrating. I also shared digs with them at Mrs Watson's place, where there were about 12 of us, all exchanging stories, but I felt left out. I knew all the players but I wasn't working with them. I had to do all my training at the Cliff on Tuesday and Thursday, which I didn't like very much, but I just had to bide my time until I was 17. The people at work were very helpful and never ribbed me about being with United.

The standard of the first team was so great in those days that the competition for places was phenomenal. Many people thought that our reserve team could have played in the First Division – that's how strong it was. I remember Matt asked Jimmy Murphy once if he had any good reserves. Jimmy told Matt that he could come and take anyone he wanted for the first team.

When I signed on with United I came under Jimmy Murphy's wing. He took me to Old Trafford on my own and spent hours and hours with me, ironing out my faults. He would pull me out of games and make me practise so that I could eliminate the faults. During matches he would bawl me out and chastise me in front of the others, but afterwards he would talk to me quietly and reassuringly. He was first-class and I know I could never have managed without him.

When I got involved with the youth side, I continually hoped to get a place in the first team alongside David Pegg and Tommy Taylor. The three of us were great friends as we all came from mining communities. Although we were in different digs we used to see each other a lot and I often spent great times with Mrs Pegg and family.

Because people like Tommy and Dennis were prone to

injury, I eventually got my first game. I received my call-up papers for National Service about the same time as I made the first team, which really frustrated me. These were great times for United and there I was stuck in an army camp! It was bad enough to be doing National Service without missing out on everything at Old Trafford. But I was still playing 14 or 15 games a year when people dropped out through injury. I played my first game against Charlton Athletic and scored a couple of goals. I had been warned that First Division football was tough, but I was well prepared for it. But it was a lot faster than the reserve side, even though I had had a good apprenticeship and plenty of encouragement.

I remember the first leg of the European Cup in Spain against Real Madrid. I was only a spectator but I realised then that I had never seen football played at that level. Even the great stadium was awe-inspiring, let alone the football.

Because things were not going so well just before the crash Matt pulled a lot of recognised players out and put some of us in the first team, players like Kenny Morgans and myself. It was the first time that I had been picked for my own sake rather than as a replacement. We started to get some good results. You see, Matt had a ruthless streak when he wanted – he had dropped players before in his early days. It was a tough policy.

This happy period was really knocked on the head by the crash – all other problems, like whether I could keep my place, were incidental. It has been a totally different journey since the crash. They were a fantastic team to play for and we were a very happy club. Even though David, Tommy and myself were all playing for the same positions, we'd always arrange to meet at the same place on Saturday night. There was no bitterness. It was just being a part of a great football world that was opening up in Europe. I could see the time when we would have filled a stadium with 200,000 people. It was a phenomenal period. Then of course there was that great game against Arsenal. That was our last before Munich. The one good thing about the disaster was that the last thing people would remember was this particular match – it was a great advert for the game. We all walked off arm in arm. It had been total attacking football. The club at that time was fantastic.

When people ask me about Duncan I feel terrible trying to explain to them how good he was. They just expect to be able to see what he was like on television – but they're never going to see it. You've only got to ask people who saw him play to realise how great he was. You see, he didn't have a fault.

To belong to United before the crash gave me some of the happiest and most exciting moments in my life. We were a remarkable side who were on the threshold of greatness; everything was before us. Even the Munich crash could not take that from us, for United still progressed and achieved greatness. It just took a little longer.

BOBBY CHARLTON

Born: Ashington, 11 October 1937
League Debut: v Charlton Athletic (Old Trafford),
  6 October 1956
Full International Debut: v Scotland (Glasgow), 19
  April 1958

Playing record with Manchester United

Season	Football League		FA Cup		European Cup	
	Games	*Goals*	*Games*	*Goals*	*Games*	*Goals*
1956–57	14	10	2	1	1	1
1957–58	21	8	7	5	2	3
1958–59	38	29	1			
1959–60	37	17	3	3		
1960–61	39	21	3			
1961–62	37	8	6	2		
1962–63	28	7	6	2		
1963–64	40	9	7	2		
1964–65	41	10	7			
1965–66	38	16	7		8	2
1966–67	42	12	2			
1967–68	41	15	2	1	9	2
1968–69	32	5	6		8	2
1969–70	40	12	9	1		
1970–71	42	5	2			
1971–72	40	8	7	2		
1972–73	34	6	1			
Total	604	198	78	19	28	10

Playing record with England

1957–58 v Scotland (1), Portugal (2), Yugoslavia

1958–59 v Northern Ireland (2), Russia (1), Wales, Scotland (1), Italy (1), Brazil, Peru, Mexico, USA

1959–60 v Wales, Sweden (1), Scotland (1), Yugoslavia, Spain, Hungary

1960–61 v Northern Ireland (1), Luxembourg (3), Spain, Wales (1), Scotland, Mexico (3), Portugal, Italy, Austria

1961–62 v Luxembourg (2), Wales, Portugal, Northern Ireland (1), Austria, Scotland, Switzerland, Peru, Hungary, Argentina (1), Bulgaria, Brazil

1962–63 v France, Scotland, Brazil, Czechoslovakia (1), East Germany (1), Switzerland (3)

1963–64 v Wales (1), Rest of the World, Northern Ireland, Scotland, Uruguay, Portugal (1), Republic of Ireland, United States of America (sub) (1), Brazil, Argentina

1964–65 v Northern Ireland, Holland, Scotland (1)

1965–66 v Wales, Austria (1), Northern Ireland, Spain, West Germany, Scotland (1), Yugoslavia (1), Finland, Norway, Poland, Uruguay, Mexico (1), France, Argentina, Portugal (2), West Germany

1966–67 v Northern Ireland, Czechoslovakia, Wales (1), Scotland

1967–68 v Wales (1), Northern Ireland (1), Russia, Scotland, Spain (1), Sweden (1), Yugoslavia, Russia (1)

1968–69 v Romania, Bulgaria, Northern Ireland, Wales (1), Scotland, Mexico, Brazil

1969–70 v Holland, Portugal, Wales, Northern Ireland
(1), Colombia (1), Equador, Romania, Brazil,
Czechoslovakia, West Germany

Goals scored are in brackets.

Also played in the Football League for:

Preston North End

JIMMY MURPHY

Assistant Manager

'I am sure that half our successes in our early days in Europe can be attributed to Jimmy's approach to us prior to a game.'

HARRY GREGG

Jimmy Murphy was from the coal-black Rhondda Valley. He was born of a Welsh mother and an Irish father, and had the fire and lyricism of those passionate people. His ambition always was to be a professional footballer, joining West Brom at 15. With them he played against all the great footballers of the day – giants like Dixie Dean, Ted Drake, Alex James and Matt Busby. The war interrupted his career and he was made to forsake the grass of West Bromwich for three years for the sand of the Western Desert with the Eighth Army.

After the war, Jimmy met up with Matt Busby who invited him to become his assistant at Manchester United. Thus began a legendary partnership that has seen no equal in British football. Out of the ruins of the badly bombed Old Trafford, they created the immortal side that was to win the FA Cup in 1948. What a team they put together: Crompton; Carey, Aston; Anderson, Chilton, Cockburn; Delaney, Morris, Rowley, Pearson, Mitten.

Although this was a wonderful team, its members were somewhat on the mature side and Busby and Murphy were well aware of the need to bring in younger players. There was very little money available for purchasing proven quality players so it was decided to find the best schoolboy footballers that 'head gardener' Jimmy Murphy could nurture to maturity.

This was a terrific challenge for Jimmy, who was to spot the boys and bring them to United fresh from school. They would then be looked after by carefully selected landladies who took them in very much as part of their own families. This family atmosphere was built up within the club to create a secure basis for these fresh-faced lads to develop their football talents and character. Jimmy and Matt asserted a friendly but firm hand upon these young players. It was a unique formula which, as history shows, produced some of the most memorable names football has ever known. This 'family' brought up such players as Duncan Edwards, Bobby Charlton, Roger Byrne, Dennis Viollet and Eddie Colman, to name but five. Finding such young, and at that time unknown, youngsters cost the club remarkably little. The five players mentioned above cost only £50 in signing-on fees.

Jimmy had two masterly assistants: Bert Whalley as team coach, and Joe Armstrong, the highly intuitive chief scout. Joe spotted Bobby Charlton when he was 15. With their youth team winning everything, they began to see the rewards of their patience.

Jimmy was the perfect man to put into practice Matt's

far-sighted philosophy – for what was emerging from this 'family' were the Busby Babes. A glance at United's position in the league during this early period gives some indication of what was grown in the Manchester United garden, reinforced by some astute, though more expensive, signings in the form of the indomitable Tommy Taylor (£29,999), Johnny Berry (£25,000), and Ray Wood (£6,000).

LEAGUE RECORD

SEASON	POSITION
1950–51	Second
1951–52	First
1952–53	Eighth
1953–54	Fourth
1954–55	Fifth
1955–56	First
1956–57	First

It became apparent that the adage 'as ye sow, so shall ye reap' was to prove apt in the case of Busby's and Murphy's philosophy.

In 1957 United failed narrowly to win the FA Cup Final and entered Europe, proving themselves against some of the most formidable sides on the Continent. They reached the European Cup semi-final in 1956–57 but were beaten by the experienced and powerful Real Madrid side, and the following year they reached the semi-final in the same competition after drawing with Red Star in Belgrade. It speaks volumes for the strength of United's reserves that after the decimation of the team at Munich they could still field a team a few weeks later strong enough to defeat the all-conquering Milan at Old Trafford.

Until the tragedy Jimmy Murphy and his assistants had nurtured their team, expecting (and doubtless deserving) success in the early 1960s. Alas, Munich was to change all that. Jimmy remembered the happy times with affection.

'One thing the army did for me was give me discipline. I had been in charge of a rest camp in Italy after spending three and a half years in the Western Desert. It was here that I met Matt again and was offered the chance to be his assistant at Manchester United. Six months later, after the war ended, I joined him and was for the first year in charge of the side which won the Central League. Matt came to my house for a drink in celebration of that success and told me I had done a remarkable job. I told him that although I was delighted with the result I didn't feel that we had anyone in the reserves good enough to justify a place on the first team. It was then we hit on our youth policy.

'I was lucky in having a terrific assistant in Bert Whalley, and he and I set out to find our young team whom we coached until they blossomed. The old players of 1948 now began to give way to the brilliant boys we managed to find over the ensuing three years. This 'new look' team began to develop not only as good club footballers but as world-class players. Bert Whalley did a magnificent job during this time, being a talented coach and a great judge of football, and was ready to help in anything both on and off the field. It was a sad and personal loss when he died at Munich.

'At the time of the Red Star game I was away from Manchester managing the Welsh team who were playing against Israel in Cardiff. When I returned to Manchester

I had not heard about the crash. I remember going into the office and asking Alma George, our secretary, if she would like a drink. She suddenly burst into tears and I asked her what the matter was. All she said was, "The plane has crashed." The horror of those words will haunt me for ever.

'I began to call anyone who might have more news. Gradually our supporters began to gather outside the ground to discover the names of those wonderful boys who had died. Slowly the news began to come in that we had lost Roger, Eddie, Billy, Tommy, Geoff, Mark and David. We had also lost Walter Crickmer, Tom Curry and dear Bert Whalley, and Matt was critically ill. It did not seem possible. I was at the ground until four o'clock that morning and when I returned home I realised that I would have to reconcile my grief and carry on alone.

'Fortunately that year we had a strong Central League side and we called upon many of them that season. Some of them were young lads not really ready but with Ernie Taylor's help and with those survivors who could play, we made it to the Cup Final. Ernie Taylor was a man of vast experience and I was grateful I could rely on his help. And, of course, Harry Gregg and Bill Foulkes did a terrific job – it was good having a few senior players around me.

'I went to Munich as soon as I could and visited the hospital where all our young lads were being looked after. I remember looking in on Duncan, who smiled at me and said, "What time do we kick off on Saturday, Jimmy?" Duncan was like that. He was in our first team at the age of 16, all the more remarkable because we had so many great players here at that time. He was also the youngest player to be capped for England and I am sure that he could have continued playing into his fifties, gaining more caps even than Bobby Charlton. He never tired of the game – a great, good, living lad. He was the most complete player I had ever seen. Men like Matthews and Finney were brilliant footballers but could really play only in their own position; Duncan could play anywhere. It was desperate that we lost him but it was a credit to his strength that even lying so ill in hospital he could joke about playing again in a few days. He valiantly hung on to life for two weeks afterwards but even his great resolve was not enough to pull him through.

'All those lads made up the most wonderful team I have seen. In my time I think we had three really great teams here, but they were the best. They could have won anything they put their minds to: the boat race, the Grand National and the Derby, anything. Nowadays football seems to be all upside down. I squirm to think how much modern players cost. Millions. And I think of what we put together for mere pennies. It was not easy and we can pride ourselves on the talents we produced here.

'Eddie Colman would have been a star in his own right at any time. He was a small player, only nine stone six pounds, but could do anything with a football. He could make the sun dance with the ball. Tommy Taylor would, I am sure, have become a second Tommy Lawton. David Pegg and Geoff Bent were magnificent then and would fit without any difficultly into any modern side today. Dear Billy Whelan would have gone on for years and I am sure would have got another 50 caps. I believe the same of that lovely, gentle, strong Mark Jones. Poor Jackie Blanchflower was a wonderful prospect, a strong and adaptable player who would have done Ireland proud for many years. When I saw Johnny Berry lying in hospital in Munich I did not think that he would survive, but I should have remembered that as a footballer he was so full of guts, fast and determined and afraid of nothing. Bad as everything was, it could have been so much worse. Some, at least, came away from the crash and Greggy, Dennis Viollet, Bobby and Bill came through to play in the final that year.

'In one way God had been very good to me. If it had not been for Wales's match with Israel I would have been sitting in Bert Whalley's seat. That was no consolation for the friends I had lost. After the crash I felt so alone – there was no one I could really talk to, as all my closest friends were either dead or injured. I really missed Bert then but I thank God I had men like Stan Crowther and Ernie, as well as the lads who'd survived, to help me. I was trying to run the club and to get a team together at the same time as travelling to Munich. I recall going in to see Matt after he regained consciousness. He took my hand and said, "Keep the flag flying, Jimmy." I did my best.

'My greatest delight over the years has, strangely, not been the winning of cups and championships, but the memory of bringing up all my youngsters. I remember them at 14 and 15, ripening like apples. One needed bags of patience and I used to cycle all over Manchester to visit them in their digs just to watch them grow. I am proud of them all.

'I remember Bill Foulkes joining up as a youngster, a big, raw-boned lad. A few people at the top didn't think he could make it. I had patience with him and proved my point because for ten seasons he was one of our stalwarts. You see, coaching is all about patience and having faith in players and giving them a fair crack of the whip. Nothing has given me more joy than seeing one of our young boys make the grade. My proudest moment was getting that battered side to Wembley – it was wonderful.

'Another proud moment was taking the Welsh team to the World Cup in Sweden. We reached the quarter-final, to be beaten by Brazil only 1–0 – and that with Pele in his prime! Mind you, we held out for 65 minutes.

'I remember once dear Duncan coming to me and saying, "Jimmy, do you mind if I buy a bike?" I said, "Okay. But be careful." I think of that wonderful footballer, the greatest of the great, cycling to the ground on a bike and, what's more, asking for my permission. This lad was an international player at 18 but was so keen on playing that he wanted to play in the Youth Cup Final for which he was eligible. We were playing against City in the final and I remember at one stage we were losing 1–0. I called Duncan and said, "Come on Duncan, we're losing." "Don't worry, son," he said, "it will be all right." Out he went for the second half and gave us two magnificent goals.

'The saddest part of the whole disaster was the day the coffins came back to United. So many people came to pay their last respects, and after all the services there was such an aura of grief in Manchester that I had to take the boys away for a breath of fresh air. So from Tuesday to Friday, every week until the Cup Final, the whole team went to Blackpool to get away from it all.

'Looking back over the years I realise what a very lucky man I have been. I have six children, one of whom played for United for a while, and 14 grandchildren, including a set of identical twins. My wife has been a wonderful support to me, though she has no interest in football –

but that's how it should be. I remember if we lost a match she would say, "Oh well, you'll win the next time." Sometimes she was right.'

Jimmy Murphy was a modest man who understood the inner world of players. He implemented Matt's philosophy and made it come to life. He found and made most of the United team. He bullied, humoured and inspired them into what they became – potentially the greatest club team of all time. There can be no more fitting tribute than that for Jimmy Murphy. Even though he retired in 1971 he was still scouting for talent up until a few days before his death on 15 November 1989.

ROGER BYRNE

'One of the things wrong with football today is that there's not the discipline and respect commanded by men like Roger.'

ALBERT SCANLON

'Roger was a class footballer. The reason he was such a good captain was that he could plan his game and therefore play instinctively.'

NAT LOFTHOUSE

Roger was signed by Manchester United in 1948 from Gorton junior side. He started out as an outside left, but his potential as a defender was very soon spotted by the club, who played him in the left-back position that he was shortly to make his own with both United and England.

Roger was a fast, stylish, intelligent master technician who had a knack for controlling the course and pace of the game. Very few wingers ever had a happy match against him. While he was very good in the air and a strong tackler, he usually preferred to keep his man in check through his astute positional play. He was a lethal penalty-taker who seldom missed and as a full back he was a man ahead of his time, invoking all his former skills and speed as a winger to make adventurous runs from his back position down the wing. Combining beautifully with Duncan Edwards he frequently initiated exciting and successful moves.

He was for a long time captain of Manchester United and once captained the England team in the absence of Billy Wright. He was a very responsible captain, at the same time being firm with the younger players but always a source of encouragement. At 28 he was the 'father' of United's Busby Babes but understood very well the frustrations of youthful players, for in his early days he himself had had an explosive temperament, being almost sent home early from a tour of South America. His early days with United were under the captaincy and guidance of a perfect gentleman, John Carey. When he took over John's mantle he took over something of his gentlemanly courteousness.

In 1955 Roger started a course in physiotherapy in the local hospital with a view to working in that field when he finally regarded himself as being too old or too slow to continue playing football. At the hospital Christmas Ball, he met another student, Joy, whom he married in June 1957. During the intervening years Roger managed to pass his preliminary and intermediate examinations, studying in the afternoons and evenings whenever he could and training with United in the mornings. During the close season he studied all day. Now remarried, Joy remembers him as an intelligent and hardworking man. At their house just outside Kendal, Joy spoke of Roger.

Roger seemed to me quite different from other people and certainly from other footballers I had come to know. He always seemed very alert, with his eyes wide open. He was a man very much with his mind on the future. I don't think he would have stayed in football after retiring as a player. He certainly would not have gone into management, although as a physiotherapist he might possibly have specialised in sporting injuries. I am told that as a youngster he was somewhat hot-headed, but I certainly never found him so.

He was one of the few full backs who could ever contain Stanley Matthews, a man for whom he had great admiration. He was a great respecter of good footballers and took on many of the qualities of the men he admired. I suppose the best of these qualities was his leadership, for he had learned, possibly from his own youth, how to keep youngsters under control. He had enormous respect for Matt, for to all those boys Matt was a god, but a very nice god. He made them all fighters. Behind Matt was a wonderful woman in Jean Busby. She was a miracle-worker.

I knew Roger only for three Februarys. The first February he drove his Morris Minor into a lamppost and fractured his collarbone. Matt was not very pleased. The second February he swerved to avoid another car and managed to crash into Matt's garden. Matt was even less pleased, particularly as he was asleep at the time. On the final February he died in the plane crash.

Eight months after Roger's death Joy gave birth to a son whom she also named Roger, in proud memory of his father. She still keeps Roger's scrapbook that he had kept since signing for United, which contains some newspaper reports from his time at the club. After Roger's debut for United against Liverpool, Matt Busby said, 'Let Byrne get the feel of things for about three First Division games and I'm prepared to say that he is certain to play for England . . . He outshone John Carey by his anticipational and positional sense, intrepid tackling and delicate use of the ball . . . The player with the perfect feet!'

According to the 'Pink 'Un', 'Byrne is 24 years of age. That gives him a long time, in normal circumstances, to remain in football.'

ROGER BYRNE

Born: Manchester, 8 September 1929
League Debut: v Liverpool (Anfield), 24 November
  1951
Full International Debut: v Scotland (Glasgow), 3 April
  1954

Playing record with Manchester United

Season	Football League		FA Cup		European Cup	
	Games	Goals	Games	Goals	Games	Goals
1951–52	24	7	1			
1952–53	40	2	4	3		
1953–54	41	3	1			
1954–55	39	2	3			
1955–56	39	3	1			
1956–57	36		6	1	8	
1957–58	26		2		6	
Total	245	17	18	4	14	

Playing record with England

1953–54 v Scotland, Yugoslavia, Hungary, Belgium,
Switzerland, Uruguay
1954–55 v Northern Ireland, Wales, West Germany,
  Scotland, France, Spain, Portugal
1955–56 v Denmark, Wales, Northern Ireland, Spain,
  Scotland, Brazil, Sweden, Finland, West Germany
1956–57 v Northern Ireland, Wales, Yugoslavia,
  Denmark, Scotland, Republic of Ireland, Denmark
1957–58 v Wales, Northern Ireland, France

GEOFF BENT

*'Geoff Bent was a great, great competitor
and excellent defender, hard as nails.'*

DENNIS VIOLLET

Geoff, who was captain of Salford Boys, was signed by United at 15. He had an opportunity to join a number of other clubs but as he was an only son, Mrs Bent decided he should go to United. Geoff was an outstanding player, strong and quick in the tackle and very difficult to beat. He could have walked into most First Division sides but at United was overshadowed by the brilliance of Roger Byrne, who commanded the position of left back. Only when Roger was injured or on international duty did Geoff find a place. He once put his frustrating position to Matt, who said, 'There are no first-team players, only first-team probables.' Geoff gave loyal and devoted service to the club and yet played only 12 first-team games. His last was against Arsenal in that glorious 5–4 victory the Saturday before Munich. He accompanied the team to Belgrade in case Roger's injuries did not respond to treatment. As history shows, Geoff watched that game and Roger played one of his finest for the club.

I talked to Geoff's wife, Marion, at her home, and she told me how she had met Geoff at the Swinton Palais when he was 17. He was then a part-time footballer and part-time joiner with the same firm that Duncan was to join later. Marion, who knew little about football, learnt about it from Mrs Bent. Geoff and Marion married in 1953. They had one daughter, Karen. She always felt part of the United family atmosphere.

GEOFF BENT

Born: Salford, 27 September 1932
League Debut: v Burnley (Turf Moor), 11 December
    1954

Playing record with Manchester United

Season	Football League	
	Games	*Goals*
1954–55	2	
1955–56	4	
1956–57	6	
Total	**12**	

TOMMY TAYLOR

'Anyone who let Tommy Taylor run into
position was very foolish.'

BILL FOULKES

'When he was playing you needn't have
bothered looking for the ball. You merely
looked for Tommy – he was never
far away from it.'

ALBERT SCANLON

Tommy was brought from Barnsley to play for United because they needed a strong centre forward to work alongside Dennis Viollet. United had been searching the country for months for what they wanted, yet there was Tommy only 50 miles away, banging in the goals for Barnsley. But banging in goals was nothing new to him. He had been, since a kid, playing on rough pitches against men twice his size and still scoring goals. Oddly, he was small for his age and only grew to his full size during his National Service. United were not alone in wanting to sign Tommy; there were 20 other clubs after him. At the end of much negotiation, Barnsley eventually sold their dark-haired and raw-boned golden boy for £29,999. Busby was anxious not to impose a £30,000 millstone around the lad's neck, so he gave the girl who'd served tea during the discussion the odd £1 for a tip. Jimmy Murphy recalled that Tommy's only request at the time of his signing was for complimentary tickets for his family. He was the most expensive player Busby had bought up until then but was to repay his fee many times over.

The late Johnny Carey told me a story that gives a good picture of Tommy in his early days. Carey had been injured and Busby asked him to go to Barnsley to have a look at Tommy. What Carey saw so impressed him that he rushed back to Busby, thinking that he was the first to discover this vein of gold. He excitedly gave his views to Busby, who said, 'I'm glad you liked him. You're the ninth person I've sent to see him so he must be good!'

Tommy was signed the following week and Carey met him at the station, where, in full view of the reporters and cameramen, Tommy appeared carrying his boots in a brown paper bag!

Tommy was an immediate success. His strength, length of stride, variation of pace and amazing head work made him one of the most feared centre forwards of all time. He had the ability to leap high for the ball and appear to hang in the air before cracking the ball with his broad forehead towards the goal. For corner kicks he would wait menacingly on the far corner of the box and begin his deadly run as the ball was kicked. Few centre halves were able to watch the ball, being too intimidated by this powerhouse charging towards them, totally committed to putting the ball into the back of the net. A glance at his goal record shows how dynamic a player he was, scoring 128 goals in 189 games. During his entire career playing for England he was only twice on the losing side.

For all his power, Tommy did not play an orthodox centre-forward game but, in keeping with many other United players, would roam out to the wing, preferably the right, to search for the ball or create confusion among the strict two-three-five formation the other teams often played. With the menacing Berry and Viollet able to slip into the centre, he would often wander out and exchange roles. It was a move like this that brought United that wonderful last goal in the quarter-final of the European Cup against Bilbao. With the score at 2–0 United were therefore level on aggregate with Bilbao at 5–5.

Tommy cut to the right and appeared to be going to have a crack at goal when he passed calmly to Johnny Berry, who had moved into the centre-forward position. Tommy's pass was hammered home. However, this tendency to wander to the wings probably prevented him reaching greater heights as an international, because Stanley Matthews commanded the right wing and he was not overkeen to change his role.

Tommy did not have delicate footwork but could hang on to a ball tenaciously and use his speed and powerful body movement to beat his opponents. His skill with his feet was mainly in his distribution and in the accuracy and power of his shot.

One of his greatest games was his last against Red Star in Belgrade, when Tommy showed his great skills and stamina and was a constant inspiration to his team.

'Tucker' Taylor – so called after his uncle, who was also

called 'Tucker' – belongs to the élite band of players whose names will always be recalled when one speaks of great footballers. Tommy lived for football and was totally dedicated to the game. At the beginning of each season he would begin his training at Old Trafford two weeks before anybody else. He had recovered from a bad knee injury and was totally fit again and could have looked forward to over ten years of top-class football.

I asked his old schoolfriend Harry England, who had seen Tommy play so many times, how good he really was. 'I'll tell you,' he said. 'One day we couldn't get a football so we played with a rugger ball and Tommy could still run rings around us. And they say he wasn't good with his feet! As for his heading, I saw him head the ball in against Huddersfield from outside the penalty area and that was the goal that gave United the league championship. That's how good Tommy Taylor was. Good? He was bloody great!'

TOMMY TAYLOR

Born: Barnsley, 29 January 1932
League Debut: (for United) v Preston North End (Old
  Trafford), 7 March 1953
Full International Debut: v Argentina (Buenos Aires),
  17 May 1953

Playing record with Manchester United

Season	Football League		FA Cup		European Cup	
	Games	Goals	Games	Goals	Games	Goals
1952–53	11	7				
1953–54	35	22	1	1		
1954–55	30	20	1			
1955–56	33	25	1			
1956–57	32	22	4	4	8	8
1957–58	25	16	2		6	3
Total	166	112	9	5	14	11

Playing record with England

1952–53 v Argentina, Chile (1), Uruguay (1)
1953–54 v Belgium, Switzerland
1955–56 v Scotland, Brazil (2), Sweden, Finland, West
  Germany
1956–57 v Northern Ireland, Yugoslavia (sub),
  Denmark (3), Republic of Ireland (3), Denmark (2)
1957–58 v Wales, Northern Ireland, France (2)

Goals scored are in brackets.

Also played in the Football League for:

Barnsley

LIAM (BILLY) WHELAN

*'He always looked slow and cumbersome,
but he was very deceptive. In training
he always managed to come first
in the mile run.'*

BILL FOULKES

'He never knew just how good he was.'

ALBERT SCANLON

Liam was born on 1 April 1935, the fourth child in a family of seven. As a young boy he spent hours playing football with a tennis ball and apart from soccer was extremely talented in hurling and Gaelic football. He joined Home Farm Football Club as a centre forward when he was 12 years old and represented Ireland at youth level. Although a brilliant schoolboy footballer, not one professional club approached him until a Manchester United scout, who was watching another boy in the same match, switched his attentions to Liam.

When he arrived in Manchester Liam went into lodgings

with Bobby Charlton, with whom he became very close, but despite this and other friendships, and despite his love of football, he became very homesick. He was not keen on close-season tours and all the time preferred to be home with his family and friends in Dublin. He was essentially a family man who wanted to settle down and run a small business in his home town. Whenever he got home he would soon be out on the streets playing football with the local children. His brother remembers that however long he had been away, as soon as he was home he would be off to the shops for a ball and playing with the kids as if he had never left. Whichever ground United played on there were always plenty of Irish supporters who would turn up to watch. Liam always delighted in spending as much time as possible talking to them.

He was a particularly devout Roman Catholic, attending church every Sunday and never without his rosary. He used to try and set a fine example to the other Irish boys at Old Trafford. Liam developed a strong tie with the local priest, the Revd Mulholland at Saint Sebastian's, Manchester, and this led to rumours that he might undertake the priesthood. These were dispelled when he announced his engagement to Ruby McCullough, to whom he was to be married in the June following Munich. Anticipating the crash on the third attempt to take off, Liam said, 'If this is the end, I am ready for it.' His brother, Christy, says that many priests in Ireland used his last words as a theme for their sermons.

As a player he shared with John White of Spurs a unique talent. He had a gift not always discernible from the terraces. He was a players' player and one had to be on the field with him to realise just how good he was. He had great mastery of the ball, hugging it to him as though he possessed it, and seemed to glide past players with ease. He had little speed and minimal body swerve and yet somehow managed to elude even the most experienced defenders.

One of his greatest games was when he played for Ireland against England and was matched against Duncan Edwards. It is recorded that both had a brilliant game. On his return to Ireland shortly afterwards, he scored two goals for Manchester United to knock Shamrock Rovers out of the European Cup. He made his league debut for United against Preston at Deepdale and in his next game, against Sheffield United, he scored his first goal. He said of it, 'What a feeling I had, something I could never hope to describe; it seemed I would burst with happiness.' In a match against Chelsea he scored from a David Pegg cross which he described in his quiet Dublin brogue: 'I hit the ball with just about every ounce of strength I could muster. The timing was excellent and the ball whizzed into the net from 20 yards like a red-hot hornet.'

His greatest goal was in the first leg against Bilbao in the European Cup. United were losing 5–2 with only five minutes to go and it was vital that United reduce the lead. Liam gathered a pass from Duncan in his own half and set out towards the Bilbao goal in what can only be described as an inspired run. He covered 40 yards through the slush and snow and eluded some fearsome tackles. Matt Busby from the bench was now on his feet, continually urging him to shoot. But Liam, the quiet genius, continued to beat man after man before drawing out the agile Carmelo and powering an unstoppable shot into the back of the net. It was a rare, memorable and significant goal, as United were to win the return match 3–0 and thus go through on aggregate.

This quiet man was something of an enigma. With most of the great players who died at Munich, one could conceivably see where their potential would lead them. With Liam it was different. He never quite realised how good he was and was, as Albert Scanlon said, embarrassed by his own talent. There are many however who believe that this gentle Irishman would have been one of the greatest of all footballers.

LIAM WHELAN

Born: Dublin, 1 April 1935
League Debut: v Preston North End (Deepdale),
    20 March 1955
Full International Debut: v Holland

Playing record with Manchester United

Season	Football League		FA Cup		European Cup	
	Games	*Goals*	*Games*	*Goals*	*Games*	*Goals*
1954–55	7	1				
1955–56	13	4				
1956–57	39	26	6	4	8	3
1957–58	20	12			3	3
Total	79	43	6	4	11	6

Playing record with the Republic of Ireland

1955–56 v Holland
1956–57 v Denmark, England, England

EDDIE COLMAN

'The creative genius of the team.'
BILLY WRIGHT

*'Eddie could put the ball in front of you,
alongside you, chip it over you. He could
do anything with it.'*
DENNIS VIOLLET

Albert Scanlon walked with me from his home in order to direct me to Eddie Colman's father's flat. We talked a lot about Eddie: about his cheerfulness; his boyish ways; his confidence as a player; his mock job as a rat catcher in the army; his duffle coat and cap – the hallmarks of Eddie Colman.

I was met at the lift door by Mr Colman and his sister. Sitting in their flat he told me about the pleasure he felt watching Eddie in his first game against Bolton and how Eddie, when faced with the advancing Nat Lofthouse, just put his foot on the ball and moved in one direction while Lofthouse went the other. 'Gifted, you see – he was gifted,' Mr Colman said, smiling. Mr Colman's one disappointment was that due to the fog he didn't see Eddie score his only goal for United against Red Star. He spoke quietly about Eddie's death. They'd heard the news but nothing had been confirmed about Eddie. However, he knew that he always sat with Mark and Tommy and their deaths had been confirmed. They went that evening to their local church and prayed. At midnight the man from the local shop that had the only telephone in the area came across to tell them. At Eddie's funeral thousands turned out and, as Mr Colman put it, they had to close the gates. After the funeral, a few of Eddie's possessions which had been recovered from the aircraft were returned to Mr Colman. They were his wallet with a few pounds in it. In a paper bag was also an apple, an orange, a quarter of tea and two pounds of sugar that his mother had packed for him.

Sometimes Matt Busby had to think a great deal before signing on a lad who had been recommended to him. With Eddie there was no doubt at all. Matt could see that this pint-sized round-faced lad with a cheeky smile was destined for greatness. He considered him to be one of the finest wing halves he had ever seen. Eddie was spotted by Matt and Jimmy in a game between Stockport Boys and Salford Boys. After ten minutes they had both agreed that he had a future with United – and maybe United had a future with him. What impressed them most was Eddie's ability to collect a ball and pass it with what Matt called 'an indefinable inherent brilliance which no amount of coaching could provide'. He was a natural: brave, resourceful and, for a small lad, highly competitive. His parents, who lived in Archie Street (which later became television's Coronation Street), did not consider him the star of the Salford team and were somewhat overcome by Matt Busby's enthusiasm. Mr Colman said to him, 'All I want is a future for my son. If you are sure he has a future as a footballer, he can certainly join Manchester United.'

Very soon Eddie became an outstanding member of the youth team. What was immediately apparent was his confidence with the ball. He would roll it, stroke it, shield it and torment players who tried to take it away from him. He could almost make it talk. What he seldom did was strike it hard, but he did not need to because of his uncanny accuracy.

Eddie's debut for United was at Burnden Park against Bolton, and it is interesting to read Nat Lofthouse's account, elsewhere in this book, of the contest between the 'Lion of Vienna' and the little lad from Salford. After that match Henry Rose, who was to die with Eddie at Munich, wrote of his debut, 'There was a lad called Colman and he's mustard!'

Jimmy Murphy once said to Eddie, 'Son, if only you would learn to shoot like Duncan you would get 20 goals a season.' Eddie replied, 'Maybe, Jimmy . . . but I'm a murderous finisher from two yards.' How right he was. In the 85 games he played Eddie scored only once and that was from two yards! It was, however, a highly signficant goal, for it was one against Red Star at United shortly before the replay in Belgrade.

Anyone who speaks of Eddie refers to him as 'Snakehips'. Matt Busby once said of Eddie, 'He's the only player in the First Division who can sell a dummy with his backside.' The press dubbed him 'Swivelhips, the player with a wiggle like Marilyn Monroe'. Joe Armstrong observed the first time he saw him, 'Put a grass skirt on him and you've got a hula-hula dancer.' Harry Gregg recalls how he used to become mesmerised by this movement and, as Eddie moved up the field, used to find himself swaying in time with him. 'I swear when Eddie waggled his hips the stanchions in the stands moved with him.'

There was, however, nothing effeminate about Eddie's movement. He was a tough tackler and it was this ability and his confidence that inspired Matt to give him the job of marking the great Alfredo di Stefano of Real Madrid in the European Cup. It was a fascinating confrontation from which Eddie emerged with great credit.

Eddie's great friends were David Pegg, Tommy Taylor and Duncan. They often went together to dances or spent evenings playing records. He often used to pull Duncan's leg about the great difference in size between the two men, and he used to enjoy dancing with Duncan's girlfriend Molly. On the field, however, it was the sorely tried Duncan who, with Bill Foulkes, would have to help Eddie out of trouble on the rare occasion someone tried to intimidate the little man.

There is little doubt in the minds of all those who saw this remarkably creative artist that the highest honours in the game would have come his way. This lovable rogue who could make the ball talk, or as Jimmy Murphy said, 'make the sun dance', died a few weeks after completing his National Service. He was barely 21.

Eddie's father spoke of the day his son's coffin was brought to the house. He knew that there had been some problems with identifying some of the bodies in Munich but he was given a sad reassurance. Eddie's dog had been waiting every day at the corner of the street for his master to return. As soon as the coffin was brought into the house, the dog ran in and sat underneath it. Eddie had come home.

EDDIE COLMAN

Born: Salford, 1 November 1936
League Debut: v Bolton Wanderers (Burnden Park),
   12 November 1955

Playing record with Manchester United

Season	Football League		FA Cup		European Cup	
	Games	*Goals*	*Games*	*Goals*	*Games*	*Goals*
1955–56	25		1			
1956–57	36	1	6		8	
1957–58	24		2		5	
Total	**85**	**1**	**9**		**13**	

DAVID PEGG

'David Pegg would always have been an asset to any team because he was a natural left-flank player.'

MATT BUSBY

David Pegg was born in Highfield near Doncaster and even as a schoolboy was a brilliant footballer. He was spotted early by a referee who was also a selector for Yorkshire Schoolboys, for whom David later played. At 14 he got his first international cap for England Schoolboys and he played alongside Duncan Edwards. Matt signed him for £10 at the age of 15½. His mother, Jessie Pegg, recalled how anxious she was about him leaving school but she told me how Matt said he'd gamble his life that David would make a professional.

David was undoubtedly one of Matt's most astute buys. He moved into digs in Manchester and was looked after by Mrs Watson, who took in United lads. He started training as a draughtsman and Mrs Pegg told of how one of the older men on the firm befriended him and used to feed him milk and cornflakes to build him up! He gained considerable experience in the highly successful youth team, and in December 1952, when David was 17, he signed professional forms. In an article he wrote, David described that day:

> It was a Friday and the team sheet seemed to take longer to come down than usual. When it was eventually posted on the board I wandered over. I looked and was a bit dejected that I had not been selected for the reserve side. Then my eye glanced to the first-team sheet and I had been selected for the first team alongside my idols – and me only 17!

He struck up a friendship with Dennis, Bobby and Tommy, who all used to come across to Manchester to visit Mr and Mrs Pegg and their two daughters. Like all those lads, he delighted in the pop music of that time. He was very keen on Nat King Cole and Frank Sinatra. He was essentially modest and quiet and always concerned about the game, always wanting to know how well he had played. His mother remembered how he used to read the newspaper the morning after the match.

In those days, when few households had a car, David used to arrive late on a Saturday in his Vauxhall Victor, which used to create a good impression locally. According to his sister Irene, an even bigger impression was created when Tommy Taylor would arrive in his car and leave it outside the Peggs' house! She used to polish them and smile at the envious neighbours. David was once arrested for speeding. The police officer put his head through David's window and said, 'I don't know whether I should book you for speeding or low flying!' Another time he got into trouble was with Matt, who had arranged to pick him up early for a game in the North. David was coming out of his digs with his tie in his pocket. Matt, in his typically subtle way, said, 'It's never too late and it's never to early to wear a tie!'

At 21 David won his one and only cap, against Ireland. This was after appearing in the England Under-23 team and the England B team. He had only really begun what was obviously going to be a spectacular career with United.

DAVID PEGG

Born: Adwick-le-Street, 20 September 1935
League Debut: v Middlesbrough (Old Trafford),
  6 December 1952
Full International Debut: v Republic of Ireland
  (Dublin), 19 May 1957

Playing record with Manchester United

Season	Football League		FA Cup		European Cup	
	Games	Goals	Games	Goals	Games	Goals
1952–53	19	4	2			
1953–54	9					
1954–55	6	1				
1955–56	35	9	1			
1956–57	37	6	6		8	2
1957–58	21	4		4	4	
Total	127	24	9	4	12	2

Playing record with England
1956–57 v Republic of Ireland

MARK JONES

'As gentle as a mouse off the field, but on it he was as hard as nails.'

ALBERT SCANLON

At 6ft 1½in and 14½ stone with size 11½ boots, Mark Jones was a formidable centre half – and yet the gentlest of men. A native Yorkshireman, he was spotted by Joe Armstrong playing for his local Don and Deane Boys team. Barnsley, his local team, were keen to sign him up but United moved quickly and soon the flaxen-haired lad was under the guidance of his idols Stan Pearson and Allenby Chilton, whom he was to succeed as centre half for United.

He started as a young man amidst such great names that he matured and grew confident quickly. When Chilton was picked for England, Mark made his debut for Manchester United in October 1950 against Sheffield Wednesday. He sent a telegram to his girlfriend June, later to become his wife: 'Playing in first team. Try to get there.' A bus was quickly requisitioned and all his family

161

and friends turned up to watch him. This delighted him, for he was a deep-rooted family man. I spoke with June, who has since remarried. She told me how Mark met her when they were both teenagers and she was working in a confectionery shop where he would call in for a custard tart on the way from his work as a bricklayer. They were engaged at 18 and married a year later. Their son, Garry, was only two years old when Mark was killed. A daughter, Lyn, was born four months after Mark's death.

After the wedding Mark and June moved to Manchester, where they set up home. It was a home which soon became the centre of Mark's world, from where he would leave daily in his long coat, belted at the waist, trilby hat and his pipe. Because of his pipe he was affectionately known as Dan Archer by the lads. But he enjoyed the training and the fun with the lads. Then he would be home again with Garry, his labrador Rick and his 55 budgies.

He got on well with all the other lads and was particular friends with Eddie, Jackie and David, who often stayed with him in Manchester. He cared passionately about his game and was very critical of his own playing. If he felt he had had a bad game, he would come home depressed and say, 'June, I played like a looney.' But if United had won he would burst through the door and whirl her around in his huge arms.

Mark had many disappointments in his life. He wanted to join the RAF for his National Service but was thwarted by an ear injury. His first child, a daughter, died at birth. His three great ambitions went unrealised. He wanted to play for England, he wanted to play in the Cup Final and, because of his affection for the Royal Family, he wanted to shake hands with the Duke of Edinburgh. Injury prevented him from playing in the Cup Final and therefore from shaking the Duke's hand, and although he won a reserve place for England, he sat on the bench throughout the match. There is no doubt, however, that had he lived, he would have gained a full cap.

Mark gained the distinction of being the youngest player at the time ever to play in the reserves for United. He was 16½ at the time and in 1949 this was considered to be a remarkable feat, but he had to wait patiently in the shadow of Allenby Chilton. After his first appearance, Mark had only three games in the first team that season and only two the following year. In 1953–54 he did not make the first team at all. He would arrive at the ground and ask Allenby how he was. 'Oh, bright and breezy,' would be the reply. 'I can go on for another three or four seasons!' However, on 10 March 1955 Mark made the position his own when in a match against Cardiff he established himself in the first team. Allenby Chilton was the first one in the dressing-room to congratulate him on his game.

His great quality was his dependability. He was extremely difficult to beat in the air and could move the ball upfield with great accuracy and force from either foot or from his head. He was strong in the tackle and very much the safe pivot around which the two most creative wing halves in the country could work their magic.

The 1955–56 season saw him mature. He played in every game and ended with a First Division Championship medal. His injuries against Bournemouth the following season put him out of the game for several months. Jackie Blanchflower took his place and played so well that he was selected for the 1957 Cup Final – so Mark's place in the team, which would have enabled him to satisfy two of his ambitions, was taken by the best man at his wedding.

At the start of the 1957–58 season Jackie was still in Mark's place, but in December, he was injured. Mark recovered his position and was playing better than ever when everything came to its sudden and tragic conclusion.

Mark's loss to football and his family was great indeed. He had such a zest for life and yet his concern for others came naturally to him. At home matches he would always go and see that people in wheelchairs had the view they wanted. There seemed no malice in the man. He was, in Chaucer's words, 'a verray parfit gentil Knight'.

His wife's last memory of him was of this gentle giant in his long overcoat and trilby hat, smoking his pipe walking out into an early Manchester fog still waving to her.

MARK JONES

Born: Wombwell, 15 June 1933
League Debut: v Sheffield Wednesday (Old Trafford),
   7 October 1950

Playing record with Manchester United

Season	Football League		FA Cup		European Cup	
	Games	Goals	Games	Goals	Games	Goals
1950–51	4					
1951–52	3					
1952–53	2					
1953–54						
1954–55	13					
1955–56	42	1	1			
1956–57	29		4	6		
1957–58	10		2			
Total	**103**	**1**	**7**	**6**		

DUNCAN EDWARDS

'Duncan Edwards was a colossus.'
BOBBY ROBSON

'There was only one Duncan.
He was the greatest.'
BOBBY CHARLTON

When Duncan was 11, the headmaster of his secondary school predicted that the young lad would one day play football for England. Seven short but remarkable years later, he was proved right. In those seven years, there emerged the most naturally talented footballer this country has ever seen. He was soon to captain the England Schoolboy team and was watched eagerly by every club scout in the First Division.

Manchester United were as keen to sign him as anyone else, and fortunately for them Duncan expressed a preference for United because of their policy of entertaining and creative football. Bert Whalley set off in his car to sign Duncan but unfortunately it broke down on the way and he had to hitchhike back to Manchester, where he arrived very late. Jimmy Murphy was somewhat concerned that another local club might appear to offer richer dreams to Duncan and sign him up in Bert's absence. Bert and Jimmy set off straight away in Jimmy's car and drove anxiously through the night, reaching Duncan's home at dawn. The lad was awakened and came downstairs in his pyjamas to find two very tired men waiting for him. 'What's all the fuss about,' he said. 'I've already agreed to sign for United.' He signed there and then and a signing-on fee of £10 was duly handed over.

At the age of 16 years and while still an amateur, he made his debut for United against Cardiff at Ninian Park. Two years later he became the youngest player ever to have played for England, at the age of 18 years and 183 days. He was to go on to win 18 caps for his country.

From a very early age, Duncan was a thorough professional. He understood that he had a great talent but, unlike many geniuses of football, he also realised that he must practise his craft. He spent hours alone honing his skills, seeking perfection. He was a fanatic for fitness, he did not smoke and he drank only a little. He intended to play football until he was an old man. He would probably have done so.

Duncan was just under six feet tall and weighed 13½ stone. There was not an ounce of fat on him and the muscles on his massive thighs rippled as he ran. Duncan would roll up his sleeves, hitch up his shorts and go out in search of adventure. He was a disciplined cavalier full of flair, but he always played within his own brilliantly paced rhythm. He was seldom off balance and rarely had the ball taken from him. Furthermore, he was without doubt one of the hardest strikers of the ball the game has ever seen. He could also hit the ball with tremendous power with his head, a skill he had perfected by hundreds of hours of practice. For such a large man he was extremely agile and fast both on and off the ball. He could switch play by deft passing of a long or short perfectly placed ball. He was devastating as a forward and had few equals in front of goal. Bobby Charlton described him as 'the greatest; there was only one Duncan Edwards'. Jimmy Murphy, whose accolades you had to earn, called Duncan the most complete player he had ever seen.

Duncan was the stuff that dreams are made of. He was as close to perfection as a footballer as it is possible to be, and many of his goals are legendary – his mighty shot against West Germany in 1957 was so fast it was invisible to everyone until it hit the back of the net! In an Under-23 international against Scotland, England were playing with only ten men because of an injury. Duncan was switched to centre forward and blasted four goals past a somewhat bewildered Scottish goalkeeper. In his final game in England against Arsenal, he hit a shot that was too hard even for the great Jack Kelsey to handle. It was the last goal that an excited and exhausted crowd were to see Duncan score. He left them with memories that they have treasured ever since.

The death of seven top-class players at Munich was a terrifying blow and the world held its breath in the hope that Duncan would somehow pull through. His great strength carried him through for 15 days after the crash, but his injuries were such that even Duncan was unable to carry on the fight for life. This quiet, fun-loving man dedicated his life to football. We will never again see such quicksilver magic, such talent, such guts and such a unique combination of poise and artistry in one footballer. We can only agree with Bobby Charlton – there was only one Duncan.

DUNCAN EDWARDS

Born: Dudley, 1 October 1936
League Debut: v Cardiff City (Ninian Park), 4 April 1953
Full International Debut: v Scotland (Wembley), 2 April 1955

Playing record with Manchester United

Season	Football League		FA Cup		European Cup	
	Games	Goals	Games	Goals	Games	Goals
1952–53	1					
1953–54	24		1			
1954–55	33	6	3			
1955–56	33	3				
1956–57	34	5	6	1	7	
1957–58	26	6	2		5	
Total	151	20	12	1	12	

Playing record with England

1954–55 v Scotland, France, Spain, Portugal
1955–56 v Scotland, Brazil, Sweden, Finland, West Germany (1)
1956–57 v Northern Ireland, Denmark (2), Scotland (1), Republic of Ireland, Denmark
1957–58 v Wales, Northern Ireland (1), France

Goals scored are in brackets.

OMO AND DAZ

Laundry Ladies with Manchester United

They were a wonderful bunch of lads, always lively and good fun. They were always looking for ways to play practical jokes on us. I suppose it was because we were the only two girls on the ground at the time, apart from Alma George. They used to drop into the cellar where the laundry room was and cadge a cup of tea or a quick cigarette. They would often bring their personal laundry down to us or ask us to iron their trousers. They were just like babes to us.

What we loved about them was that they were just ordinary lads – they would catch the same bus as us, shop in the same shops and chat to the same people. They were just like workmen going about their daily jobs, not like modern players today, whom you never see. They used to rush down and tell us some lorry had come and taken all the washing away with it. Up we would rush, all concerned, but of course nothing had happened at all and

171

there the lads would be, with big grins on their faces. Sometimes we'd be carrying baskets along the corridor and Eddie would leap on us, giving us a terrific scare. He was a wonderful Salford lad – full of life.

When we went to the Cup Final on the train, everyone who lived near the railway line waved a towel or tablecloth as we sped past. Even though we were beaten in 1958 after Munich and everyone was very disappointed, they were still there waving to greet us on our way back.

Duncan Edwards was one of our favourites and always seemed older than his years. It seemed extraordinary that he was in the first team at the age of 16. It was not until one saw him training on his own that one realised how dedicated and great a player he was. On the whitewashed wall outside he would make a mark and he would spend hours relentlessly striking the ball at the same spot. Every ball hit was to the same place. He would vary the pace but always maintain accuracy.

Mark Jones was a lovely boy, so quiet and gentle. He used to come to the ground with his shotgun and dog to shoot the pigeons which were always a nuisance. He would take them to a lady close to the ground who used to make pigeon pie.

In those days people used to come on their bikes to the game and many of the houses nearby used to take in the bikes at three old pence a go. Many rents were paid that way. The bikes used to be taken inside and put anywhere, even in the lounge.

We had a radio in the laundry room, and the Monday before the crash, the lads came down to hear the draw for the cup. Eddie brought some towels he wanted us to wash and Ray was upset because Harry was going to be goalkeeper against Red Star. We wished them all the best and that was the last we saw of so many of them. It seemed so wrong and such a waste to lose them. We loved them all.

A very sad day followed shortly afterwards, when the coffins arrived and were laid out in the gymnasium. We went down there to dust and polish them. That was the saddest day of our lives, dusting the coffins of lads who so little time ago had been playing hide and seek in our laundry. We went to a different funeral each day to say goodbye to our friends, and although it was good to see Harry and Bill and later Bobby and some of the others as they were released from hospital, it was never the same again. Although there were some good lads who came to United later, the spirit seemed to go out of the club and for us never really returned.

BOBBY ROBSON

Fulham, West Brom and England

My first international match, against France at Wembley in 1957, was the last international match before the Manchester United air crash, and in that match I played alongside 'Busby Babes' Duncan Edwards, Tommy Taylor and Roger Byrne. We won 4–0: I scored two goals and Tommy Taylor scored two.

Really, that was my first opportunity to get to know them as people, rather than just as opponents, and they had that lovely combination of being super fellows as well as masterful players.

Duncan Edwards was a colossus, and if he had lived would, I think, have broken the record number of England caps. He was certainly in the same stratum as Bobby Charlton, Bobby Moore, Billy Wright – perhaps the best ever. He was physically strong, had great power, a good football brain, ability both on the ground and in the air, he was fast – in fact, he was a complete player.

175

I played alongside Tommy Taylor – in the old terminology he was a centre forward, I was an inside right – and we both scored two that day.

Tommy was a traditional English centre forward, who was approaching Tommy Lawton's class in the air, his greatest strength. He had a nice shape to his game. Having established himself in the Manchester United first team and although a relative newcomer to the side, he would have played a long time for England.

Byrne was a stylish defender, very neat and tidy in his control of the ball, a very quick player who was emerging as a sound full back who could rapidly convert defence into attack by really accurate use of the ball, or by bringing the ball through himself at speed.

These are my personal recollections of the playing abilities of these three men. Only four months after that match they were dead.

My greatest memory of Manchester United as a team is that in the same month as that international, November 1957, they came to West Brom where I was playing, and we won a fantastic game 4–3. I scored twice in a match where the attacking gifts of both teams outweighed the defensive talents of both. I put that match down as one of the three best I have ever played in my life. It was fast, flowing, attacking, positive football, played with a great competitive edge, but absolutely sportingly clean. It was the sort of match to which one would want to take a friend who had never seen any football, for his first taste of the sport.

Manchester United were a terrifically skilful side with a tremendous future. They could have dominated the league during that era in the same way that Liverpool dominated the '80s. They had a great combination of speed, strength and skill, and had great variety in their play. They had a great shape to their game from which two vital elements emerged – they had width and penetration. With their combination of experience and youth they were, in my opinion, going to be unstoppable for some time to come. The crash that decimated the team was, without doubt, football's greatest tragedy.

NAT LOFTHOUSE

Bolton Wanderers and England

The Manchester United team of the 1950s was to me one of the greatest teams ever in Britain, if not the world. I remember in 1956 in Berlin seeing what I think must be the finest goal I have ever seen. Reg Matthews, our goalkeeper, threw the ball to Duncan Edwards about 30 yards outside our penalty area. Duncan turned on the ball, beating one German; he then ran with the ball to the half-way line where he was taken on by another, whom he passed. Just inside the German half he was tackled again by yet another but still came out with the ball. When he was only about 15 yards inside the German half all he did was kick the ball. There were 80,000 people in that stadium and not one of them knew where the ball had gone until the net bulged. They were still cheering that goal even after the Germans had kicked off to restart the game. It was a totally unbelievable goal.

I remember that evening we were celebrating our 3–1 victory and I was drinking some pretty strong German wine with Tom Finney, Roger Byrne, Dennis Wilshaw and Duncan. I told Duncan to go easy on the wine as it was a bit more potent than anything we were used to. Duncan said, 'Oh, I'll be all right' but we finished up having to take him to the lavatory. He was in a bad way but we all reckoned he had earned his little celebration.

Tommy Taylor was brilliant in the air and came on the international scene in 1953–54 when we played in South America. We played together and kept it wide and I think it worried a few sides out there! We couldn't beat them on the ground but we could get them in if the ball was 20 feet high!

Eddie Colman played his first game for United against Bolton. He was wing half in that game. He had the ball and I was chasing after him. I was an international then and here was a young lad playing in his first big match. Even so he sent me one way and went off with the ball in another direction. I thought, 'You little bugger,' but I couldn't catch him.

I shall always remember Roger Byrne as a class footballer. He used to think about everything he did and plan his game. I think the reason he was such a good captain was that he could plan his game and therefore play instinctively and keep an eye on what everybody else was doing.

Duncan had a natural talent and was one of the most gifted of all players. It was very difficult playing against him because he was so powerful but so agile. I am quite a big guy myself but Duncan used to make me look about as agile as an elephant. Not just me but a lot of other guys too. He was a supreme player. I used to look at that team and think what a perfect combination of players it was. They had Eddie Colman, who was such a crafty player, Mark Jones, who could stop anything, and Duncan, who could do just about everything. They were hard to play. You could tackle Mark, but if there was the slightest danger of you getting the better of him he would simply give it to Duncan. Even if one managed to get past these guys there was still Harry Gregg to contend with. What a hell of a guy he is, not just on the field but off it too. When you have a guy like that who climbed back into a burning plane to help his friends, you've said it all.

They were clever devils too, because they even had their own massage oil which you could smell 100 yards from the ground! You thought, this is it, this is United. United was always THE game.

I remember we played Manchester United 16 days before Munich and they thrashed us 7–2. I got a goal in the last minute when I charged Harry – I think the ref gave it out of sympathy. We all sat later drinking Double Diamond in the dressing-room.

I remember hearing the news about the crash. We had a pub in those days and I was there when we heard about it on the six o'clock news. The whole place was stunned – but then the news stunned the whole of Britain, and nearly killed half the North. I found it very hard to believe. I still miss them. They were great guys, all of them.

NORMAN WILLIAMS

A Supporter

*'The trouble with us old ones – we've
seen the best. We've seen football
played with passion.'*

ERIC GIBBS AND PAT McGEE,
MANCHESTER UNITED SUPPORTERS

I have been a Manchester United supporter all my life
but the greatest team we have ever had were the Busby
Babes before Munich. I remember them all vividly and
can recall highlights of many of those matches better
than I can remember those of the last few years. It was
wonderful to watch that United side.

I particularly remember one match against Wolver-
hampton Wanderers. With only ten minutes to go to the
final whistle we were losing 3–1 and many people were
leaving the ground early, disappointed. Suddenly United
scored and then two or three minutes before the end of
the match, they managed to equalise. Just seconds before
the whistle they slotted in their fourth and winning goal.

It was incredible. I remember going back to the coach where everyone who had left early was grumbling about losing 3–1. They wouldn't believe me when I told them we had won 4–3.

I can't remember who scored all the goals but I remember Mark Jones, at centre half, getting at least one of them. He was the sort of centre half you don't see these days. He was a wonderful header of the ball and used to meet almost everything in the air. I have often seen him head the ball from the 18-yard line right into the other half. I believe he could head the ball just as far as many could kick it.

I remember another fantastic game of the Busby Babes against a very experienced Chelsea team on a very heavy pitch. I was sure that in such heavy going our young team would have great difficulty and, indeed, by half-time Chelsea were ahead by two goals to nil. However, in the second half United came back with a brand of football that was all their own and proceeded to take Chelsea apart, winning 4–2.

Yet another incredible game was one played against Arsenal. Arsenal scored within the first few minutes and I remember one newspaper reporter saying that this was the worst thing they could have done, for it spurred United into a frenzy of wonderful football. They paralysed Arsenal for the rest of the match, coming away the winners by six goals to two.

There was another famous match with Arsenal on the Saturday before Munich. United, playing away, were leading 3–0 but in the second half Arsenal bounced back, scoring three goals in quick succession to equalise. United went ahead once more through Viollet and Tommy Taylor scored the fifth, only for Arsenal to pull another goal back to end a great nine-goal thriller.

There were other cliffhanger games like that and I particularly remember one at Hartlepool where United had been leading 3–0 but at the final whistle came away winners by four goals to three.

That team had everything. It had fluency, poise, ability and power, but one of the outstanding assets of the team was its togetherness. All these youngsters were good friends and all the supporters felt very close to the players. I remember travelling down to London by train and Eddie Colman – known affectionately as 'Snakehips' – bringing a crate of ale into the compartment for the fans. It is very different today because footballers are so highly paid that they are no longer part of the working class, and therefore there is no longer the close affinity between the players and the fans that there was then.

I remember the first time Duncan Edwards played for United. He was only 16 at the time and United lost that particular match 4–1. But I remember, after Duncan scored from the penalty spot, thinking that here was going to be a great player. The power of his kick sent the ball almost invisibly into the back of the net.

I remember Billy Whelan, who to me was one of the greatest of all ball-players. For all-round ability I think Best was probably better, but for sheer skill I would put Whelan ahead because he had no pace; it was sheer skill on the ball that ensured his success. There was that famous match against Bilbao on a snow-covered turf at Maine Road when Billy went through the entire defence. Matt Busby was screaming at him from the bench to pass the ball but Billy just went on and on through the defence and put the ball in the net.

There was a bunch of us who used to go together to all

the matches in the '50s and stand by the side of the tunnel next to the goalposts at the Stretford End and sing. Nothing obscene as there is today. At half-time we would make our way to the other end – tricky with a crowd of 60,000! – and continue our songs during the second half.

I remember yet another match in which we beat Blackpool to win the league championship. Blackpool had earlier beaten us 2–1 at Old Trafford but this time United paralysed them with football they had never seen before. But it was a strange match when it was very hard to get the ball in the net, especially since Blackpool kept passing the ball back to their own goalkeeper. However, perseverance proved to be the order of the day and we came away with the match and the championship.

I remember being at London Road station when Tommy Taylor arrived from Barnsley to play for United. He was carrying his football boots under his arm and a United official greeted him, saying, 'Oh go on Tommy, we don't do that here. You don't carry your gear at Old Trafford; we do that for you.' Tommy was a £30,000 signing. Actually, Matt Busby paid £29,999, because he said he did not want him to have a £30,000 tag on his head.

Tommy was one of the greatest centre forwards of all time and I remember a particular incident concerning him. Henry Rose, a *Daily Express* sports writer, who sadly died at Munich, wrote an article stating: 'If Tommy Taylor is the best centre forward in the country, I'm Father Christmas.' On New Year's Day in 1957 Tommy Taylor scored a hat-trick against Chelsea at Old Trafford, and the following morning the *Daily Express* featured a photograph of Henry Rose complete with

Santa Claus coat and beard, as though to say 'You've won, Tommy'.

Tommy and Johnny Berry had a great understanding for one another on the field. I remember how Johnny used to go down the wing taking on man after man before crossing the ball to exactly the spot where Tommy could take it with his head. They must have been telepathic.

David Pegg was another great player, though from a different mould. He was slower than Berry but a much better dribbler. David could beat players through skill; Johnny beat them through sheer pace. Another player famed for his speed, not only physical but mental too, was Dennis Viollet. Dennis was a brilliant goal-poacher, always managing to be in the right spot at the right time – and usually before any of the opposition knew he was there. He was the essence of quick movement and quick shooting.

Roger Byrne was the first full back with pace. In the '50s full backs were supposed to be strong men whose job was basically to boot the ball as far up the field as possible. But Roger brought a certain grace and character to the full-back position. He had started with United as a forward in 1952 and had helped them to win their first post-war championship, but Matt Busby had other ideas and converted him into a left full back. He was full back for England for a long time and I am sure that had he lived he would have been the England captain after Billy Wright. He was a great captain for United and had a great influence on the team. I remember the steadying influence he had in the Bilbao match at Maine Road without which United might have failed to win. It needed a very cool head. United were leading with only five minutes to go when Billy Foulkes made a mess of a back pass to Ray Wood. Things went to pieces for a moment but Roger stepped in and got everyone together again. He was the skipper and what he said, in no uncertain terms, was law.

Despite his mistake in that match, Billy Foulkes was a very good full back who later made his mark as a centre half after Munich and went on with United to win the championship and, of course, the European Cup, in which he scored the vital goal in the semi-final. However, for me, the best centre half since the war was without doubt Mark Jones. He was quite brilliant and I am sure would have played regularly for England. He was a great guy off the field too. I met him at a supporters' club 'do' and I always remember him. At Christmas 1957 we went to another supporters' club 'do' to which he had given one or two supporters a lift in his little Ford Popular. I remember he said, 'Do you like the leopard skin seats? I shot 'em myself!'

I'll never forget the tragedy of that crash. We were all so close to the team that it felt as though we had lost members of our own families, and I remember being in tears on hearing the news. I have never been ashamed of admitting that. I went to the memorial service for the team and that proved to be a very sad occasion. It was desperate to lose so many young players who had such promise. I am sure that they would have become one of the greatest football teams of all time.

THE NEW DAWN

'The road back may be long and hard but with the memory of those who died at Munich, of their stirring achievements and wonderful sportsmanship ever with us, Manchester United will rise again.'

H.P. HARDMAN,
CHAIRMAN MANCHESTER UNITED, 19 FEB 1958

Many thought that after the crash United would never be the same again. They had not reckoned, however, with the indomitable courage of Matt Busby, nor with the personal courage of the survivors, nor with the spirit of those young reserves who were thrust straight from their incompleted apprenticeship into the first team. Nor had they reckoned with the intuition and inspiration of Jimmy Murphy, who was able to mould from this assortment of inexperienced youth and shaken survivors a team that was able to play again 13 days after the crash. This team, with the assistance of new signings Ernie Taylor and Stan Crowther, created the most electrifying night Old

Trafford has ever seen. This ragtag and bobtail team found inspiration from the magnificent crowd. In quite the most unbelievable of games, United destroyed Sheffield Wednesday. No side anywhere could have beaten United that night.

Jimmy Murphy had brought together men of magic that night. Far away in Munich Matt Busby lay in hospital, still gravely ill. But his spirit was at Old Trafford and always will be.

During the next ten years the Manchester United phoenix arose from the ashes of the crash and in 1968 Matt, Jimmy, Bill Foulkes and Bobby Charlton were to weep once again – but this time for joy. In the stands, sharing those emotions, were the players who had survived the crash. That night Manchester United had won the European Cup.